Your Castle: Dream Home Or Nightmare?

Your Castle: Dream Home Or Nightmare?

BY

Charles A. Herman

A guide in evaluating the advantages (and disadvantages) of purchasing a house; questions prospective buyers need to be asking themselves before making the purchase; financial requirements; step-by-step guide to purchasing or building a house; special house design considerations for comfort, safety and security; and financial guidance during a crisis

eBookstand Books
www.ebookstand.com
www.cyberread.com

Published by
eBookstand Books
Division of CyberRead, Inc.
1909_5

Copyright © 2005 by Charles A. Herman
All rights reserved. No part of this publication may be reproduced or transmitted in any form or by any means, electronic or mechanical, including photocopy, recording, or any information storage and retrieval system, without permission in writing from the copyright owner.

ISBN 1-58909-238-4

Printed in the United States of America

CONTENTS

Acknowledgements iii

Preface v

Chapter 1 1
    Purchase Or Rent A House - Which Is Best??

Table 1 3
    Typical Expenses Incurred In Purchasing An Existing $180,000 House With A 10% Down Payment

Table 2 9
    How To Determine The Maximum Monthly Mortgage Payment Allowed By A Mortgage Company

Table 3 12
    Thirty Year Mortgage For A Given Monthly Payment And Interest Rate

Table 4 18
    Typical Expenses Incurred In Selling A House Purchased For $180,000 Two Years Earlier

Table 5 19
    Total Cost To Purchase A $180,000 House And Own It For Two Years

Chapter 2 25
    Total Financial Analysis

Table 6 29
    Total Future Financial Analysis

Chapter 3 33
    Current Financial Budget

Table 7 37
    Current Financial Budget

Table 8 44	
Monthly Budget Expense Form	
Table 9 45	
Monthly Budget Expense Form	
Table 10 47	
Monthly Budget Expense Form	
Table 11 48	
Monthly Budget Expense Form	
Table 12 50	
Monthly Budget Expense Form	
Table 13 51	
Savings For Anticipated Future Expenses	
Chapter 4 53	
Steps To Purchasing Your House	
Chapter 5 61	
Steps To Building Your House	
Chapter 6 79	
House Design Considerations	
Chapter 7 109	
Safety And Security	
Chapter 8 125	
The Impossible Happens: Financial Crisis	
Chapter 9 133	
Heads I Win; Tails You Lose	
Chapter 10 143	
Summary	
Appendix 145	
Index 157	
Glossary 161	

ACKNOWLEDGEMENTS

There is a realtor in Georgia, two real estate people in Indiana, and a family house builder in Indiana who have made very valuable contributions to this book. Their assistance has made this book possible. I would like very much to identify them and thank them for their contributions.

Unfortunately, identifying these fine, honest, hard-working people could well bring the wrath of less-than-honest realtors, appraisers, mortgage companies and banks upon them. Consequently, they will remain unidentified.

You wonderful people know who you are. You are not only people with whom I have done real estate business with, you are highly valued friends. I will make it a point to personally be in contact with each of you.

Perhaps, through this book with your contributions, and the splendid examples you are setting in the housing industry, a slight improvement in the legal and ethical standards of the housing industry will take place. Above all, house buyers will be informed of how to purchase their house with minimal risk of being scammed or facing financial hardship.

PREFACE

In 2000, there were about 119,628,000 houses in the United States. In 2000, 6,213,000 houses were purchased. For some, their house was a "dream home" and a source of great joy. In the same year, though, approximately 100,000 families experienced the nightmare of losing their house to foreclosure. Many hundreds of thousands more families were threatened with foreclosure, had poorly and/or fraudulently constructed houses that required expensive repairs, or suffered with predatory mortgages, but had the financial resources to escape foreclosure – in some cases, only temporarily – and to bear the heavy financial burdens of repairing their poorly constructed houses and predatory mortgages.

This book is written for all people who own a house, or are considering purchasing a house, or are planning to build a new house. It guides the reader through all the steps that need to be taken prior to purchasing or building a house in order for their house to have the best chance of becoming a "dream home" and not a nightmare. The reader is shown how to evaluate whether they should purchase a house or rent one; how to evaluate their financial position and the appropriate house price for them; financial steps to take before buying a house; and factors to consider before purchasing or building a house.

Though this book is not intended to design a house for the reader, two chapters are devoted to often overlooked design considerations and safety and security features which will reduce the cost of ownership and provide greater enjoyment, safety and comfort to the owners. Many of the design considerations and safety and security features presented can be incorporated into an existing house as well as a new house, making the book very valuable to current house owners.

One chapter is devoted to guiding a homeowner through a financial crisis. Though following the steps presented in this book will minimize the likelihood of a financial crisis, a serious illness, loss of a job, etc. can cause this to happen.

This book is designed to enable you to obtain the house of your choosing and to enjoy your "dream home" with maximum comfort, safety and security while minimizing costs and the risks of poor or fraudulent house construction, predatory mortgages and foreclosure.

CHAPTER 1

PURCHASE OR RENT A HOUSE - WHICH IS BEST??

Owning your own home is the dream of many Americans. It is often a wise decision to invest in a house. Sometimes, though, it is wisest to *not* purchase a house, but to rent a house or apartment.

A house is usually the largest investment made by a person during their life. It is complex, very expensive and time consuming to purchase a house. It is also complex, very expensive and time consuming to sell a house. A wise person will look very carefully and objectively at his or her financial position; the economy, both locally and nationally; their long range plans; the community in general; and the specific area where they would like to live before deciding to purchase a house. And once they decide to purchase a house, the wise buyer will assemble a team of experts to assist them.

Questions that potential house buyers should ask themselves before purchasing are shown below.

1. Am I financially able to purchase a house?

Purchasing a house normally requires good credit, and a significant amount of cash money. The first step should be to obtain a copy of your credit report. Examine it carefully to be sure it is accurate, and no credit activities are missing. If there are any errors, report them in writing immediately to the credit bureau. If there is anything derogatory in the report (such as an open judgment against you or an overdue payment outstanding), take care of it immediately. Then follow up in two months with a request for another credit report to verify that your credit report has been corrected. Check it to be sure anything derogatory in the report has been changed to show appropriate payments have been made, and that any omissions have been corrected.

Having a good credit report is very important. A credit report which shows slow payments on financial obligations or open judgments will result in mortgage companies not offering you a mortgage, or substantially increasing the down payment requirement and/or the interest rate.

Table 1 shows it will typically require more than $28,780 cash up front to purchase a $180,000 house with a 10% down payment.

TABLE 1

TYPICAL EXPENSES INCURRED IN PURCHASING AN EXISTING $180,000 HOUSE WITH A 10% DOWN PAYMENT[1]

Settlement Charges

Loan origination fee to a broker (typically 3% of loan)	$4,860
Appraisal fee	$300
Administration fee to mortgage company (typically 1.6% of loan)	$2,592
Interest on mortgage (from date of closing to date mortgage payments are in effect) (15 days with an 8% mortgage interest rate was used for this example)	$533
Closing fee for title company	$250
Closing attorney fee	$400
Title insurance (typically 0.64% of sale price)	$1,151
Miscellaneous title company charges	$46
Recording fees for mortgage and deed	$52

Other Expenses

House inspector fee (estimated) (for the house inspector you select to inspect the house)	$300
Attorney fees (estimated) (for your personal attorney)	$300
Total Expenses Incurred At Time Of Purchase	$10,784
Down payment (10% of purchase price is used for this example)	$18,000
Total Cash Outlay To Purchase House	$28,784

---

[1] *The expenses shown are typical expenses incurred in the purchase of a house. There are other expenses which may also be charged, depending upon your locality and the agreement negotiated with the realtor(s), mortgage company and the seller.*

There are ways of reducing the initial expenditure in purchasing a house – such as purchasing a house with no down payment, and eliminating your house inspector and personal attorney. Eliminating the down payment, though, usually results in an increased interest rate on the mortgage and sharply increased monthly payments (see also Veterans Administration Guaranteed Loans on page 103).

Eliminating your house inspector and personal attorney may save a small amount of money during the purchase. But eliminating them is highly likely to cost you much more than you would save. Without them, you will be the *only* person involved in the purchase whose objective is to look out for your interests. It must be remembered the selling realtor is an agent for the seller. They make money by selling the house – and the higher the price, the more they can make. The mortgage company is interested in loaning you as much money as possible and at the highest interest rate possible in order to maximize their profits – but limited by financial formulas that control *their* risk to an acceptable level. Some have been known to add junk fees to their closing charges, such as "document preparation" (which involves only pushing a few keys on a computer keyboard and costs them nothing) and charging $150 for a credit search (while their actual cost is $15). And the closing attorney is essentially a clerk whose function is to review all documents to be sure they have been properly signed, proper payments made to the seller, realtor, appraiser, etc. and to protect the interests of the mortgage company.

This is not to say all realtors, mortgage companies, closing attorneys and sellers are crooks out to skin you. Many of them are very fair and honest – but a few are wolves in sheep's clothes. Most, if not all, of these four or five people involved in selling a house to you will be strangers (that is, people you have known for less than two months). It is in their best interest to get as much money from you as possible, and to avoid disclosing anything (at least as much as the law allows) which would make you want to reduce the amount of your offer or to cancel your purchasing the house. Do you really want to face these expert real estate strangers alone, or would you also like some experts working with you, negotiating hard for you, and looking out for your best interest? Obviously, the latter is the best choice.

An example case of what happened to a young couple in Fort Wayne, Indiana will bring home the point.

A young couple with children was shopping for a house. They found a house they liked, and proceeded to purchase it. They did so without having the house inspected by their own house inspector and without the assistance of their own attorney.

Shortly after purchasing the house, the basement flooded with water. When they mentioned this to a neighbor, the neighbor said the previous owner also had problems with the basement flooding.

Since this had not been disclosed prior to the purchase, the new owners of the house filed a law suit against the former owner and the realtor. The Court, however, ruled in favor of the former owner and realtor because the new owner had not asked anyone prior to the purchase if there was any problem with flooding in the basement. However, if the realtor or former owner had been asked about flooding in the basement, they would have been required to disclose this problem. Had the realtor or former owner failed to answer the question honestly, the new owners would have had a good fraud case against the realtor and/or former owner.

If the new owners had used the services of their own house inspector and attorney, they most likely would have learned of this problem in advance, and certainly would have taken legal steps to protect themselves prior to purchasing the house.

The price of a house is usually negotiable. Any reduction you can negotiate in price may also mean a reduction in the down payment. Sometimes, a realtor, or the broker of the loan, or the mortgage company will also be willing to negotiate their fees. Though the realtor is paid by the seller of the property (not the buyer), the realtor will sometimes negotiate a lower fee with the seller, especially if only the realtor who has listed the house is involved in the transaction. This can enable the seller to reduce the sale price to the purchaser, but still receive nearly the same amount of money.

It is wise to explore these possibilities. After all, the fees paid to the above three businesses as a result of your purchasing a $180,000 house will normally be $10,800 to the realtor (6% of the sale price); about $4,860 to the broker for the loan origination fee (3% of the loan); and about $2,592 to the mortgage company for an administration fee (1.6% of the loan).

For example, if you can negotiate a 25% reduction of these fees (which total $18,252), you will save $4,563 cash at the time you purchase your house. Sometimes a buyer will be able to negotiate a larger cost reduction than this, while other times a buyer will be able to negotiate only a small cost reduction. It depends on how badly they want to sell to you and how skilled you and your attorney are at negotiating.

Sometimes, a seller will be willing to pay some of the closing costs that you as a buyer would normally pay. If so, you can place a clause in your offer, such as, "Seller to pay up to 5% of purchase price towards Buyer's closing costs and prepaid expenses." For the $180,000 house shown in Table 1, this would have saved the buyer $9,000 at closing. Although this is an expense to the seller, it is a relatively "painless" expense since the seller never has to take money out of their pocket. The seller's proceeds will simply be reduced by the amount stipulated.

2. How much can I afford to pay for a house?

Mortgage companies generally require the ratio of monthly debt payments to monthly gross income to be less than 35% to 41%, depending upon the economy, your credit rating, the size of your down payment, etc. Monthly debt payments include payments for: automobiles; house; bank loans; boats; alimony; child support; court judgments; credit cards; job related expenses (union dues, child care, etc.). It does not include daily living expenses or any personal obligations you may have, such as a loan from a family member.

To determine the maximum monthly house payment that a mortgage company will approve, complete Table 2 with the appropriate financial data for you.

The next question is what is the price of the house that can be purchased with this monthly payment. That is determined by (1) the number of years of life for the mortgage and (2) the interest rate.

It is recommended that the mortgage be for thirty years. This will make the monthly payments lower than for a shorter term mortgage. If you are financially able to pay more than the monthly mortgage payment for a thirty year mortgage for the house you have chosen, you may pay an additional amount on the principal each month. This will cause your mortgage to be paid off earlier than planned and will reduce your interest expense.

The interest rate can be estimated by calling several mortgage companies and asking them what their rates are for the house you are considering and your credit and income position. They will tell you that you are _pre-qualified_ for a mortgage of a certain amount and at a specified interest rate. This _does not_ guarantee that the mortgage company will provide this mortgage. It is only an estimate based upon the information you provide them.

Table 3 shows the allowable thirty year mortgage for a given allowable monthly mortgage principal and interest payment and a given mortgage interest rate. For example, if the maximum allowable monthly mortgage principal and interest payment is $600 and the interest rate quoted by the mortgage company is 7%, the maximum amount of the mortgage will be $90,090. If the maximum allowable monthly mortgage principal and interest payment is $1,500 and the interest rate is 10%, the maximum amount of the mortgage will be $170,940.

TABLE 2

HOW TO DETERMINE THE MAXIMUM MONTHLY MORTGAGE PAYMENT ALLOWED BY A MORTGAGE COMPANY

1. Determine your gross monthly income
   (income before any deductions) $_____

2. Determine your total monthly payments:

Automobile loans	$_____
Payments on any other mortgages	$_____
Monthly payments on all bank loans	$_____
Total monthly payments on credit cards	$_____
Monthly payment on boat, airplane, etc.	$_____
Monthly alimony payment	$_____
Monthly child support payment	$_____
Monthly payment on court judgments	$_____
Monthly union dues	$_____
Monthly child care payments	$_____
TOTAL MONTHLY OBLIGATIONS	$_____

If mortgage company requires monthly payment / gross income ratio to be 35% or less, then maximum allowable monthly mortgage payment = (.35) x (gross monthly income) − (total monthly obligations).

If mortgage company requires monthly payment / gross income ratio to be 41% or less, then maximum allowable monthly mortgage payment = (.41) x (gross monthly income) − (total monthly obligations).

Example case

A family has a gross weekly income of $1,200. Their monthly payments are:

Automobile loan	$250
Payment on lake cottage mortgage	$500
Payment on bank loans (no bank loans)	None
Monthly credit card payments	$200
Monthly boat payment	$250
Monthly alimony payment	None
Monthly child support payment	None
Monthly payment on court judgments	None
Monthly union dues	$ 50
Monthly child care payments	<u>$250</u>
TOTAL MONTHLY OBLIGATIONS:	$1,500

Monthly gross income = ($1,200/week) x (52 weeks per year) / (12 months per year) = $5,200.

If the maximum monthly payment to gross income ratio is 35%, maximum allowable mortgage principal and interest payment = (.35) x ($5,200) - $1,500 = $1,820 - $1,500 = $320 per month.

If the maximum monthly payment to gross income ratio is 41%, maximum allowable mortgage principal and interest payment = (.41) x ($5,200) - $1,500 = $2,132 - $1,500 = $632 per month.

Caution: If you have other financial obligations which are not considered as monthly financial obligations by a mortgage company (such as a personal loan from a relative), or anticipate other financial obligations in the near future (such as medical bills, college for children, etc.), a total financial analysis must be prepared to assure that you will have adequate funds available. See Chapter 2, Total Financial Analysis.

TABLE 3
THIRTY YEAR MORTGAGE FOR A GIVEN MONTHLY PAYMENT AND INTEREST RATE

Maximum Allowable
Monthly Mortgage
Payment For Principal and Interest

Mortgage Interest Rate

	6%	7%	8%	9%	10%	11%	12%
400	66,670	60,060	54,510	49,690			
500	83,330	75,070	68,140	62,110	56,980	52,500	
600	100,000	90,090	81,770	74,530	68,380	63,000	58,500
700	116,670	105,110	95,390	86,960	79,770	73,500	68,250
800	133,330	120,120	109,120	99,380	91,170	84,000	78,000
900	150,000	135,140	122,650	111,800	102,560	94,500	87,750
1,000	166,670	150,150	136,280	124,220	113,960	105,000	97,490
1,100	183,330	165,170	149,910	136,650	125,360	115,500	107,240
1,200	200,000	180,180	163,530	149,070	136,750	126,000	116,990
1,300	216,670	195,200	177,160	161,490	148,150	136,500	126,740
1,400	233,330	210,210	190,790	173,910	159,540	147,000	136,490
1,500	250,000	225,230	204,420	186,340	170,940	157,500	146,240
1,600	266,670	240,240	218,040	198,760	182,340	168,000	155,990
1,700	283,330	255,260	231,670	211,180	193,730	178,500	165,740
1,800	300,000	270,270	245,300	223,600	205,130	189,000	175,490
1,900	316,670	285,290	258,930	236,030	216,520	199,500	185,240
2,000	333,330	300,300	272,550	248,450	227,920	210,000	194,990

TABLE 3
(Continued)

THIRTY YEAR MORTGAGE FOR A GIVEN MONTHLY PAYMENT AND INTEREST RATE

Maximum Allowable Monthly Mortgage Payment For Principal and Interest

Mortgage Interest Rate

	6%	7%	8%	9%	10%	11%	12%
2,100	350,000	315,320	286,180	260,870	239,320	220,500	204,740
2,200	366,670	330,330	299,810	273,290	250,710	231,000	214,490
2,300	383,330	345,350	313,440	285,710	262,110	241,500	224,240
2,400	400,000	360,360	327,070	298,140	273,500	252,000	233,990
2,500	416,670	375,380	340,690	310,560	284,900	262,500	243,740
2,600	433,330	390,390	354,320	322,980	296,300	273,000	253,490
2,700	450,000	405,410	367,950	335,400	307,690	283,490	263,240
2,800	466,670	420,420	381,580	347,830	319,090	293,990	272,980
2,900	483,330	435,440	395,200	360,250	330,480	304,490	282,730
3,000	500,000	450,450	408,830	372,670	341,880	314,990	292,480
3,100	516,670	465,470	422,460	385,090	353,280	325,490	302,230
3,200	533,330	480,480	436,090	397,520	364,670	335,990	311,980
3,300	550,000	495,500	449,710	409,940	376,070	346,490	321,730
3,400	566,670	510,510	463,340	422,360	387,460	356,990	331,480
3,500	583,330	525,530	476,970	434,780	398,860	367,490	341,230

3. What is the state of the economy – both nationally and in your community?

If the local economy is strong, the demand for houses may be high, making the selling prices high. If the national economy is strong and house sales nationally are strong, there will be a high demand for mortgages. You may also find the interest rate on mortgages high. Hence, you may face a high sales price (which will require a larger down payment) coupled with high mortgage interest rates (which will result in high monthly payments). If you are financially able to purchase a house under these conditions, and your income will be secure for at least the next three years and you do not plan to move within this period, it may be safe to do so. You must recognize, though, that adverse economic conditions within the next three years could make the value of your house decline to a value lower than your purchase price. If you would have to sell the house in this period, you may be forced to sell it for substantially less than you paid for it. Since there would also be substantial costs incurred in selling your house, you may find it necessary to *pay out a substantial amount of money in order to sell your house during this period.*

If the local economy is weak with low housing demand while the national economy is strong, house prices will probably be reduced. If you are financially able to purchase a house and are reasonably certain you will be financially secure and will keep your house for at least the next three years, it may be wise to purchase a house.

If the local and national economy are both weak, house prices and mortgage interest rates may be low, making the purchase of a house look very attractive. However, you should look very carefully at your present financial position, and at the anticipated financial position for at least the next three years. Although you presently may be financially capable of purchasing a house, if there is danger of your losing your source of income within the next three years, purchasing a house would not be wise. The loss of income shortly after purchasing a house could easily result in your being unable to pay the monthly mortgage payments and result in the mortgage company foreclosing on your house.

If the local economy is strong but the national economy is weak, extreme care should be exercised before purchasing a house. You may face a "seller's market", meaning house prices will be high. There may be danger of the national economy pulling down the local economy. If this occurs, it could cause you to lose your job and be unable to pay the monthly mortgage payments in the future. If, however, you are financially able to purchase a house and are reasonably certain of being financially secure and not moving for more than three years, it may be safe to buy.

4. Will I live in the house for at least three years?

As mentioned previously, purchasing and selling a house are very expensive. A home buyer who sells their house within three years of purchasing it will usually lose money. In fact, they may have to *pay money in order to sell it*. It may also require several months to sell a house. During this period, the homeowner will need to continue paying mortgage payments, insurance, taxes, utilities, paying for repairs and maintenance, etc.

Table 1 shows the typical costs associated with purchasing a $180,000 house. Table 4 presents the typical selling expenses for this house two years later. Table 5 shows it will *cost the homeowner $48,855 to own this house for just two years!* On a monthly basis, this is $2,036 per month.[2]

---

[2] *These expenses do not take into consideration the income tax savings that may be available to a house owner. This will vary from one homeowner to another. However, it does not change the basic premise, which is that it is more economical to rent a house for three years than to own one for this period of time and then sell it.*

A house often has a rental rate of about 1% of its market value. Thus, you could rent a $180,000 house for about $1,800 per month. You would save about $236 per month by renting instead of buying this house for two years. Over two years, your savings would be about $5,664.

In addition to being more economical to rent a house for three years than to own it, renting will also provide you greater flexibility when you move, and much greater peace of mind. When you leave a rented house, the expenses for the house stop – or perhaps may continue for a short period, depending upon the rental agreement with the owner of the house. At worst, they will be for a small amount of money and for a short time. When you leave a house that you own, the expenses for the monthly mortgage payment, insurance, utilities, maintenance, taxes, etc. continue as long as you own the house. It may well be a large, undefined expense that will continue for an indefinite time. If it does not sell quickly, it could mean financial ruin for you.

As an example, suppose your company offers you a promotion to a new position three years after you purchase your house, and the position is in a city 200 miles away. If you accept the promotion, you may have to start working in your new position before your house is sold. It could take several months – possibly a year in rare circumstances – to sell your house. Consequently, you could easily find yourself in the position of owning the house in your old location and living where your new job is located at the same time. This would require that you continue paying the mortgage payments, insurance, utilities, taxes, maintenance, etc. on your old house while also incurring the costs of living in your new location. In essence, this would be like paying for two houses at the same time – a fete few people are financially able to do.

If you have owned your house for more than three years, you will have substantial equity in it. You will also have had an opportunity to save money for more than three years since incurring the expenses of purchasing your house. These savings will enable you to weather the expenses of maintaining your old house for several months (if it does not sell immediately) when you move to your new location. And the sale of your old house should provide you with cash.

Sometimes people will place their house for sale in advance of when they plan to move. This will shorten the period of owning the house after moving away. But great care must be exercised in writing the sales agreement to allow you to remain in the house as long as needed. If your house should sell quickly before you are ready to move, the new owner could insist upon immediate possession, leaving you with no place to live.

TABLE 4

TYPICAL EXPENSES INCURRED IN SELLING A HOUSE PURCHASED FOR $180,000 TWO YEARS EARLIER

Sale price of house (1)	$190,960
Commission paid to realtor (typically 6% of sale price)	$11,458
Attorney's fees	$50
Surveyor's fee	$300
Total Expenses:	$11,808

Note: (1)
Real estate usually appreciates in value over a period of time. A 3% annual appreciation rate is often considered a representative appreciation rate. For this example, a 3% annual appreciation rate has been used. Hence, 3% annual appreciation of this house over a two year period will increase its value from $180,000 to $190,960.

It should be noted that the appreciation rate for a specific house is dependent upon the economy, mortgage interest rates, the demand for houses in a locality, etc. at the time a house is purchased and when it is sold. Though the value of a house normally appreciates over a period of time, the reader must be aware that poor economic conditions may cause the value of a house _to decrease over a short period of time_. Hence, the owner of a house who is forced to sell their house within a few years of the purchase may be forced to sell their house for less than the purchase price. And needless to say, if potential buyers become aware that you are being forced to sell your house quickly, they will exert considerable pressure on you to reduce your price. Thus, a person who has owned a house for only a few years may well have to _pay out money_ in order to sell their house.

TABLE 5

TOTAL COST TO PURCHASE A $180,000 HOUSE AND OWN IT FOR TWO YEARS

Initial Expenditures At Time Of Purchase

Down payment and earnest money (10% of price)	$18,000
Total expenses incurred at time of purchase (see Table 1)	10,784
Total Expenditures At Time Of Purchase	$28,784

Expenses Incurred During The Two Year Period

Monthly payments (24 payments of $1,188.76)	$28,530	
Property tax - Varies with locality (assume tax is $3,000 per year)	$6,000	
Private mortgage insurance [1]	$1,000	
House insurance [2]	$756	
Loss of interest that could have been earned if initial expenditure money had been invested [3]	$2,199	
Repairs and maintenance (estimated)	$1,000	
	$39,485	
Total Expenditures To Own House Two Years:	**$68,269**	
Gross sale price of house:		$190,960
Less: Total expenditures to own house two years	$68,269	
Expenses incurred in selling house	$11,808	
Payoff of mortgage balance [4]	$159,738	
Total Cost To Purchase House, Own It For Two Years, and Sell It	$239,815	
Loss Incurred By Owning House Two Years ($239,815 – 190,960)		$48,855

See footnotes on next page.

Footnotes for Table 5

1. Private mortgage insurance (often abbreviated "PMI") is insurance the mortgage company usually requires a house buyer to purchase if the buyer's equity in the house is less than 20% of the purchase price. This insurance protects the *mortgage company* if the buyer defaults on the mortgage. It provides nothing for the buyer. The cost varies with the cost of the house and locality, and is usually between $300 and $1,000 per year.

If a buyer is able to provide a 20% down payment at the time of purchase, the mortgage company may not require PMI. A 20% down payment may also open the door to lower interest rates from the mortgage company. Hence, a 20% down payment will require a substantial cash outlay at the time of purchase, but will make a large reduction in your monthly payments and long term expenses.

2. The cost shown for house insurance is considered typical for a $180,000 house – that is, the cost may be more or even less. The cost of the house determines the insurance premium to a large degree. Other factors also have a large influence. Some are listed below.

A. Location Of House

If the house is located in an area where there is unusually high risk of damage (such as fire, crime, etc.), the premium will be higher.

B. Flood Protection

Homeowner's insurance usually *does not provide protection from flood damage.* If your house is located in an area where there is considered to be a risk of flood damage, the mortgage company will require you to purchase flood insurance. This insurance can be very expensive, often costing two to three times as much as regular homeowner's insurance.

C. Inflation Coverage

The value of a house and its contents normally increases with time. The insurance policy should provide for *replacement value* for your home and its contents. That is, if your home was worth $180,000 when you purchased it and it is destroyed two years later and it requires more than $180,000 to replace it, the insurance company will fully pay for replacement less the deductible amount on the policy. However, there may be policies available that do not provide replacement value protection. These policies provide you with less protection, and may have slightly lower premiums. The premium savings, though, is not considered worth the loss in insurance coverage.

D. Deductible Amount

All insurance policies provide for the home owner to be responsible for a certain amount of damage to the house. This is called the *deductible amount.* The deductible dollar value is your choice. You can usually choose a deductible amount from about $250 to more than $1,000. If you choose $250 deductible insurance, you will be required to pay the first $250 of any claim for damages, and the insurance company will pay the remaining balance. Similarly, if you choose $1,000 deductible insurance, you will be required to pay the first $1,000 of any claim and the insurance company will pay the balance.

The insurance premium decreases significantly with higher deductible levels. Thus, if you will be able at any time in the future to pay for $1,000 damages to your house, you can reduce your insurance premiums by selecting $1,000 deductible insurance instead of a lower amount. On the other hand, if you will not be able to incur this much of an expense, a lower deductible amount may be best for you.

E. Premises Alarm Systems

Smoke and burglar alarm systems in a house will usually reduce insurance premiums. They are also strongly recommended for your safety. See Chapter 7, Safety And Security.

F. Age Of House

Newer houses pose less risk to insurance companies due to improved materials and building codes. Consequently, insurance companies usually offer a significant reduction in their insurance premiums.

3. If the initial expenditure of $28,784 had been invested for two years at an interest rate of 3.75% instead of being spent on the purchase of a house, this money would have earned $2,199.

4. During the first two years, payment on the principal will be $2,262, reducing the mortgage balance from the initial $162,000 to $159,738.

5. Does the community in general – and the specific location of the house I want – meet the needs of my family and me?

This is as important as the above questions you should be considering. It is fifth in the list of questions only because it would not look right if there were two #1 questions. Specifically:

A. Does the community have the cultural features that I want?
B. Does the community have the medical and religious facilities I want for my family?

C. Is the crime rate acceptable in the community, and at the house location?

D. Is the commute from the house to work a reasonable commute?

E. Is the house located near satisfactory schools for my children?

F. Is the house located on the edge of a housing addition where a business may be constructed nearby in the future – or is it within an addition surrounded by houses?

Your employer, coworkers, the newspaper, church, bank, the community police department, the county police department, your architect, attorney, realtor and house inspector can help to provide some of the answers to these questions. But it may well require a year or more of your living in a community before you can objectively and fully answer all of these questions to your satisfaction. During this period, it is best for you to lease a house or apartment.

During your search for answers to the questions, you may find a house that appears to be ideal for you. There may be a strong temptation to purchase this house prior to answering all questions to your satisfaction. This must be avoided. You need to be able to answer all of the above questions to your satisfaction before committing to make the largest purchase of your life. The purchase of a house is a *major investment*, and it must be approached as such with a clear vision and sound financial planning and without rose colored glasses.

This search for answers to the questions should not be rushed through hastily or looked upon with displeasure, nor should the money spent on rent be considered as wasted. The time and effort spent on answering these questions, and money spent on rent, should be considered an investment toward purchasing the right house for you and your family. Enjoy your search for your house. Do it thoroughly and thoughtfully. The better your search is conducted, the better your house will fulfill your wishes and bring you years of happiness.

If, upon completion of finding answers to these questions, you find that it is not advisable to purchase a house at this time, don't be discouraged. You probably saved yourself from getting into a bad situation. You now know what needs to be done to enable you to safely purchase the house you desire. _Make it a goal to achieve this! Keep this goal in front of you at all times and work toward it constantly. In time, you will achieve your goal._

If, upon completion of finding answers to these questions, it appears to be advisable to purchase a house, _don't do so yet!_ You may have some expenses that the mortgage company would like to ignore in their financial analysis. This is explained in Chapter 2.

CHAPTER 2

TOTAL FINANCIAL ANALYSIS

The financial analysis prepared in Table 2 is typical of what a mortgage company wants to see. However, it is incomplete – especially if you have personal loans from relatives or friends or will soon be incurring other expenses, such as medical bills or college education expenses for children.

You may wonder why a mortgage company would knowingly work with an incomplete financial statement.[3] The answer is simple. MONEY. The mortgage company wants very much to sell you a mortgage – especially the mortgage officer who is trying to sell you a mortgage since their income is probably a percentage of their sales. They anticipate that you will do all in your power to keep current on your mortgage to avoid foreclosure, even if it means that you have to forego repaying a loan from a family member, cancel a vacation, get a second job, postpone dental or medical treatments, etc. And if a few people cannot make the mortgage payments and the mortgage company forecloses on a house, the mortgage company still wins. Private Mortgage Insurance protects mortgage companies from any losses.

---

[3] *Upon completing the financial statement for a mortgage company in Georgia for the purchase of our house, I told our loan officer there was no place on their financial statement form for a personal loan from a family member, and started to tell her I had such a loan. Before I could complete my statement, she said, "I don't want to hear about that." Since this was a private loan, there was no record of this in my credit report or anywhere else. By preventing me from disclosing it on the financial statement form, the mortgage company would know nothing about it, thereby making my financial position look stronger than it actually was. And by preventing me from telling her about it, she could claim she knew nothing about it if any problems arose later.*

For your financial security, you need to prepare a total financial analysis. Table 6 shows how to prepare a total financial analysis. This table will clearly show you what your income and expenses will be after purchasing your house.

Item 3 in Table 6 is your daily living expenses. The present owner or the utility companies can provide you with the annual utility expenses for the house you want to purchase. The remaining expenses can be determined by itemizing your expenses for a few months. Simply carry a small notebook with you at all times and write down everything you purchase immediately when you make each purchase. Do not wait until later when it may be more convenient. It might be forgotten.

After subtracting all expenses (Item 5) from the total net income in Item 1, there must be a cash reserve (i.e., the cash reserve must be a positive number). The total expenses shown in Item 5 must be less than the net income shown in Item 1. If the total expenses exceed the total net income, then either the credit card debt will be increasing, or some of the bills will not get paid, or money will not be saved for the future anticipated expenses, or a combination of these. *It is a condition which must be avoided.*

There are four remedies, namely: (1) increase your net income; (2) decrease your expenses; (3) reduce the savings rate for future expenses (item 4); or (4) a combination of these three steps. People usually do not save adequately for future expenses. Hence, reducing the savings rate for future expenses should be done only as a last resort and after careful analysis of the future anticipated expenses. Decreasing expenses (Items 2 and 3) is often the easiest method and usually can be implemented most quickly. Be sure the expense reductions are reasonable. Do not reduce an expense so much that you cannot achieve it safely and with reasonable comfort. Doing so will usually result in not really achieving the reduced expenditure goals and becoming frustrated by not having the cash you expect to have at the end of each week.

Increasing your net income is also an option. Although this may be more difficult to achieve and take more time, it should be considered. Does your work merit a raise? Is overtime work available? Is a better job with better pay available? Is a part time second job possible? Pursuing these questions will be to your benefit.

It is possible you will find the financial analysis used by mortgage companies (Table 2) shows you can make monthly mortgage payments of a certain amount, while your total financial analysis (Table 6) shows the cash reserve is zero or a negative number with that mortgage payment. What does this mean?

Assuming the expenditures and net income you have entered in Table 6 are accurate, this is the most accurate financial statement. It means your current expenditures and anticipated future expenses will be exceeding your net income. There's a word for this. It's called going broke!

In addition to meeting the mortgage company's requirements in Table 2, you must also have a positive cash reserve in Table 6. If there is not a positive cash reserve, then (1) expenditures must be reduced, or (2) net income must be increased, or (3) both, in order to achieve a positive cash reserve. If careful analysis of Table 6 shows a positive cash reserve cannot be created with the purchase of a house, then the purchase of a house must be postponed. Undoubtedly, this will be frustrating. But it is better to learn this *before* you purchase a house than to purchase a house and then later run out of money.

A negative cash reserve *does not* mean that you can never purchase a house. It simply means that your expenses *at this time* will exceed your income if you were to purchase a house, and that you need to reduce your expenses, increase your income, or both, before buying your house. By developing a budget (as shown in the next chapter), you will be able to pay off some of your present obligations and save toward a larger down payment, thereby reducing your monthly expenses when you make your house purchase and making the purchase possible.

If you meet the requirements of mortgage companies in Table 2 and your cash reserve in Table 6 is a positive number, it means that you have the financial capability to purchase your house. However, the reader should carefully look over their current financial position before making this major investment. Spending a few years in preparation for the purchase of your house could save you hundreds of thousands of dollars, as shown in the next chapter.

TABLE 6

TOTAL FUTURE FINANCIAL ANALYSIS

1. Determine your net monthly income
   (all income after all deductions) $_____

2. Determine your total monthly payments:

   Automobile loans $_____

   Payments on all mortgages
   (including the house you will be buying) $_____

   Monthly payments on all bank loans $_____

   Total monthly payments on credit cards $_____

   Monthly payment on boat, airplane, etc. $_____

   Monthly alimony payment $_____

   Monthly child support payment $_____

   Monthly payment on court judgments $_____

   Monthly union dues $_____

   Monthly child care payments $_____

   Monthly payments on personal loans
   (from family, friends, etc.) $_____

   Monthly insurance payments:

       Life insurance: $_____
       Car insurance: $_____
       House insurance: $_____
       Health insurance: $_____
       Other insurance: $_____ $_____

   TOTAL MONTHLY OBLIGATIONS: $_____

TABLE 6

TOTAL FUTURE FINANCIAL ANALYSIS
(CONTINUED)

3. Determine other current monthly expenses:

Automobile operating expenses (fuel, license plates, repairs, etc.)	$_____
Church & charities	$_____
Clothing & shoes	$_____
Groceries (foods, non-alcoholic beverages, laundry supplies, soaps, shampoos, etc.)	$_____
Household (house repairs & maintenance; lawn care, etc.)	$_____
Medical bills	$_____
Miscellaneous (postage, childrens' allowances, hair cuts, road tolls, etc.)	$_____
Personal entertainment (restaurant, theater, travel, alcoholic beverages, etc.)	$_____
Telephone	$_____
Trash removal	$_____
Utilities:	
Electric: $_____ Gas: $_____	
Water and Sewage: $_____	$_____

TOTAL: $_____

TABLE 6

TOTAL FUTURE FINANCIAL ANALYSIS
(CONTINUED)

4. Anticipated future expenses which I am now saving towards monthly (monthly amounts)

Medical	$_____
College	$_____
Vacation	$_____
Retirement	$_____
Other	$_____
TOTAL:	$_____

5. TOTAL OF ITEMS 2, 3 & 4 $_____

6. CASH RESERVE
   (Item 1 – Item 5) (Must be a positive number) $_____

CHAPTER 3

CURRENT FINANCIAL BUDGET

At this time, you have probably seen all of the tables and financial numbers that you want to see. If you are one of the few people who meet the mortgage company mortgage requirements in Table 2, have a cash reserve in Table 6, very little debt (including credit cards), a good credit record, and have the cash available to pay 20% down on the house you have chosen, and at least another $20,000 cash available for closing costs and a cash reserve, and a secure income, perhaps you are ready to proceed with the purchase of your house. If you satisfy all requirements of Tables 2 and 6 and have a secure income, but have substantial debt and/or can make only a 10% down payment on your house, you may want to wait a while before purchasing your house.

Lets look at two families: Jack and Beth, and Norman and Cathy. Both families have exactly the same $25,000 debt on credit cards and car loans, credit history, etc., and the same income and living expenses. Each family is renting a house with monthly rent of $900. Both are interested in purchasing a $180,000 house. Each family has $30,000 savings in the bank.

Norman and Cathy decided to postpone the purchase of their house and to continue to live in their present house for $900 per month for three more years. They decided to make a budget to pay off their debts and save so they could make a 20% down payment when they make their house purchase. Total rent cost for three years was $32,400. And they paid off their $25,000 debt in this period.

When Norman and Cathy shopped around for a mortgage three years later, they found mortgage companies were eager to sell them a mortgage. Since they could make a 20% down payment and had no other debt, they were offered a mortgage

33

with a 7% interest rate for thirty years. And with a 20% down payment, PMI (private mortgage insurance) was not required. Consequently, their expenses for three years of renting a house and thirty years of purchasing a house was as shown below.

Rental house cost for three years ($900 / month for 36 months)	$32,400
Payoff of $25,000 debt	$25,000
Closing costs [$10,784 (from Table 1) + $36,000 down payment]	$46,784
Monthly mortgage payments for principal and interest ($144,000 mortgage at 7% interest rate for 30 years) ($959 per month from Table 3)	$345,240
Total cost for Norman and Cathy to pay off their $25,000 debt + rent for 3 years, then purchase their house over the next 30 years	$449,424

Jack and Beth decided to proceed with their house purchase immediately. They purchased their house with 10% down payment, as shown in Table 1. Total cash outlay to purchase their house was $28,784. That left them with only $1,216 cash. And they had a $25,000 debt to pay off.

Because of their high debt and low down payment, the lowest interest rate a mortgage company would offer them was 9% for a thirty year mortgage. And since their down payment was less than 20%, they had to pay PMI of $600 per year for ten years. Since their mortgage was for ($180,000 − $18,000) or $162,000, their monthly mortgage payment for principal and interest was $1,304 (Table 3). With PMI, their monthly payments for the first ten years was $1,354. The total expenses for Jack and Beth for the next 33 years is shown on the next page.

Closing costs [$10,784 (from Table 1) + $18,000 down payment]	$28,784
Payoff of $25,000 debt	$25,000
Monthly payments of principal and interest of $1,304 / month for 30 years	$469,440
Payment of PMI for ten years at $600 per year	$6,000
Property tax for 3 years [4] (assume $3,000 per year)	<u>$9,000</u>
Total cost to buy house, pay debt and pay additional property tax	$538,224

As you can see, Norman and Cathy's expenses of $449,424 were much less than Jack and Beth's expenses of $538,224. Norman and Cathy saved $88,800 by planning and budgeting before they purchased their house.

This, of course, is an example. The savings you would realize could be more or less than shown in this example. But is saving about $88,800 on the purchase of a $180,000 house of interest to you? If so, read on. It's really very simple to achieve. It requires making a budget which will:

1. Pay off most of your debts

2. Enable you to develop an excellent credit rating

3. Enable you to accumulate savings for a 20% down payment, pay closing costs, and have a cash reserve of at least $5,000 after paying all of the above expenses.

---

[4] *Since Jack and Beth owned their house for three years longer than Norman and Cathy during the 33 year period, they had to pay property tax for three more years.*

Many people shudder when they hear the word "budget". Perhaps it is because they think of pain when they hear that word, believe it will interfere with their lifestyle, or believe it is complicated. A budget is simply a financial plan. When properly prepared, it will not cause pain or interfere with a family's lifestyle, and will be very easy to use. It will enable a family to do things that would have otherwise been impossible to do, bringing them joy.

If you satisfy the requirements of Tables 2 and 6, but have substantial debt (more than 20% of your net annual income), or cannot make a 20% down payment on the house of your choice, it would be in your best interests to postpone purchasing your house for a while. Use this time to pay off your debt, or at least reduce it substantially. Use this time to save toward a 20% down payment. How do you accomplish this? That magic word – a budget. Using Table 7, it is very easy to develop a budget for your present living conditions. As you can see, it is very similar to Table 6, except for modifications to reflect your present living expenses. Complete Table 7 with your current net income and expenses. Determine each expense carefully, including those you determined by noting them in a notebook for a period of time. For each item, ask yourself, "Do I really need to spend this much? Do I want to spend this much?" If you feel some of the expenses should be reduced, or increased, do so. But make any adjustments to expenses a small amount.

TABLE 7

CURRENT FINANCIAL BUDGET

1. Determine your net monthly income $_____
   (all income after all deductions)

2. Determine your total monthly payments:

   Automobile loans $_____

   Payments on rent or mortgage
   of your present house or apartment $_____

   Total Monthly payments on all bank loans $_____

   Total monthly payments on credit cards $_____

   Monthly payment on boat, airplane, etc. $_____

   Monthly alimony payment $_____

   Monthly child support payment $_____

   Monthly payment on court judgments $_____

   Monthly union dues $_____

   Monthly child care payments $_____

   Monthly payments on personal
   loans from family, friends, etc. $_____

   Monthly insurance payments:

       Life insurance: $_____
       Car insurance: $_____
       House or renter's insurance: $_____
       Health insurance: $_____
       Other insurance: $_____ $_____

TOTAL MONTHLY PAYMENT
OBLIGATIONS: $_____

TABLE 7

**CURRENT FINANCIAL BUDGET
(CONTINUED)**

3. Determine other current monthly expenses:

    Automobile: Fuel: $_____

    Repairs, maintenance, license plates: $_____

Total	$_____
Church & charities	$_____
Clothing & shoes	$_____
Groceries (foods, non-alcoholic beverages, laundry supplies, soaps, shampoos, etc.)	$_____
Household (house repairs & maintenance; lawn care, etc.)	$_____
Medical bills	$_____
Miscellaneous (postage, children's allowances, hair cuts, road tolls, etc.)	$_____
Personal entertainment (restaurant, theater, travel, alcoholic beverages)	$_____
Telephone	$_____
Trash Removal	$_____

    Utilities:

    Electric: $_____

    Gas: $_____

Water & Sewage: $_____	$_____
TOTAL:	$_____

TABLE 7

CURRENT FINANCIAL BUDGET
(CONTINUED)

4. Anticipated future expenses which I am now saving towards monthly (monthly amounts)

Medical	$ _____
College	$ _____
Vacation	$ _____
Retirement	$ _____
Savings toward down payment on new house	$ _____
Other	$ _____
TOTAL:	$ _____

5. TOTAL OF ITEMS 2, 3 & 4 $ _____

6. CASH RESERVE
   (Item 1 – Item 5) (Must be a positive number) $ _____

After completing Table 7, Item 6 (Cash Reserve) should be a positive number. This is the surplus cash available each month. Put this surplus cash into your checking and savings accounts until their total balance is three times the dollar amount of Item 5 in Table 7. This will provide you with an emergency reserve that is exactly the amount of money you will need for three months if, for any reason, your income would stop. Though we all anticipate it will never happen to us, it does happen, often unexpectedly and because of circumstances beyond the control of a family (for example, a spouse's company eliminating their position or going out of business, illness, injury, etc.). After you have established your emergency reserve, use the cash reserve (Item 6 in Table 7) to pay off debts listed in Item 2 of Table 7, with priority given to debts with high interest rates. Credit cards typically charge very high interest rates. For example, a person with a credit card debt of $10,000 with an interest rate of 18% will be charged $150 per month in interest. In order to pay off the credit card debt, it follows naturally that use of credit cards should be avoided. Period. To do this most effectively, list each of your debts like the example below – that is, the creditor with the highest interest rate at the top; the creditor with the next highest interest rate next to the top; the creditor with the third highest interest rate third from the top; etc.

Creditor	Amount owed	Interest Rate	Comments
ABC Bank	$5,000	21%	Credit card
DEF Bank	$4,000	17%	Credit card
GHI Bank	$7,000	14%	Credit card
JKL Bank	$9,000	10%	Car loan
MNO Bank	$7,000	7%	Personal loan

ABC Bank has the highest interest rate, and is the rascal you want to pay off first. The next one you want to pay off is DEF Bank; then GHI Bank; etc. Naturally, you will need to pay the required minimum monthly payments to each of the other creditors each month.

If you have a large credit card debt and have many credit cards, you might find it impossible to avoid using any credit card and still make the required minimum monthly payments on all debts and to pay more than the minimum monthly payment to the creditor who charges the highest interest rate. If that occurs, use only the credit card with the lowest interest rate, and use it only when absolutely necessary. The key is to pay off the creditor with the highest interest rate as soon as possible, and to reduce your total debt.

Now you are ready to put your financial plan (the budget) into action. This is the easiest part of all. It involves five steps.

1. Deposit all of your income into your checking account each week (or however often you are paid).

2. From Item 3 of Table 7 (Current Monthly Expenses), add together the following expenses: automobile fuel; clothing and shoes; groceries; miscellaneous; personal entertainment. Then divide this number by 4.33 (which is the number of weeks in a month). Cash a check for this amount each week, and use this cash to pay these expenses. You and your spouse can share the responsibilities of these expenses. For example, Norman and Cathy's budget expenses may have looked something like this for each week:

Automobile fuel	Norman's car:	$15.00	Cathy's car:	$10.00
Clothing and shoes	Norman:	10.00	Cathy & children:	20.00
Groceries	Norman:	-0-	Cathy:	95.00
Miscellaneous				
Postage	Norman:	-0-	Cathy:	5.00
Childrens' allowances	Norman:	15.00	Cathy:	-0-
Hair cuts & permanents	Norman:	3.00	Cathy:	4.00
Road tolls	Norman:	5.00	Cathy:	-0-
Other	Norman:	5.00	Cathy:	5.00
Personal entertainment	Norman:	$30.00	Cathy:	$30.00
Total weekly expenses	Norman:	$83.00	Cathy:	$169.00

Norman was given $83.00 each week to take care of the expenses for fuel for his car, his clothing and shoes, children's allowances, his haircuts, road tolls, other miscellaneous expenses, and his personal entertainment. Cathy was given $169.00 each week and was responsible for taking care of the expenses of fuel for her car, clothing and shoes for herself and the children, groceries, postage, her hair care, other miscellaneous expenses, and her personal entertainment.[5]

3. All of the monthly payments in Item 2 of Table 7 are essentially fixed monthly expenses. Pay the minimum required each month on each debt, except for the debt with the highest interest rate. Payment on the debt with the highest interest rate should be as much as possible each month. For example, if the required minimum monthly payment to ABC Bank is $100, and the Cash Reserve (Item 6 in Table 7) is

---

[5] *Personal entertainment expenses are a combination of personal expenses for snacks and beverages purchased (not as part of groceries), alcoholic beverages, tobacco products, etc., as well as family expenses for dining out, theaters, etc.*

$500, pay the $100 minimum that was budgeted + $500 each month (which is a total of $600) until this debt is fully paid. Then do the same with DEF Bank, etc.

4. Make a table for the current monthly expenses (Item 3 of Table 7) which were not included in Step 2 above, as shown in Table 8 on the next page. Write the budgeted amount for each item under the word "Budget." Then as purchases are made in each category, write in the amount spent on the lines in each category immediately after making the purchase.

At the end of the month, when all of the purchases have been entered, Table 8 may look like Table 9. This is for the first month you have used your budget. The numbers shown in Table 9 are example numbers. Your budgeted amount for each item and your expenses will probably be different than shown.

TABLE 8

MONTHLY BUDGET EXPENSE FORM

MONTH_____

                                    Budget Overage Available
                                                (Under) This Mo.

CARS – MAINT – REPAIRS

_____

_____

_____

Sum for Month $

HOUSEHOLD

_____

_____

_____

Sum for Month $

MEDICAL

_____

_____

_____

Sum for Month $

UTILITIES

_____

_____

_____

Sum for Month $

TABLE 9

MONTHLY BUDGET EXPENSE FORM

MONTH ___July___

	Budget	Overage (Under)	Available This Mo.

CARS – MAINT – REPAIRS $270

Cathy's Car: Lube and Oil Change $25

Sum for Month $25.00

HOUSEHOLD $30

Gas for Mower: $3
Grass fertilizer and weed killer: $35

Sum for Month $38.00

MEDICAL $145

Cathy: Dentist $70

Sum for Month $70.00

UTILITIES $250

Gas Bill: $7
Electric Bill: $35
Water & Sewage Bill: $30

Sum for Month $72.00

Notice in Table 9 that some of the expenses for the month of July are less than the budgeted amounts, while other expenses are more than the budgeted amounts. This is perfectly normal for any one given month.

Table 10 is the budget sheet for the month of August. Note that the budgeted amount for Cars – Maintenance & Repairs remains at $270. However, only $25 was spent in July. That is $245 under the budget. So ($245) is written under the words "Overage (Under)". Since last month's expenditure was $245 under budget, this amount is added to the $270 budgeted for the month ($270 + $245 = $515), and is written under the words "Available This Month". This is the actual amount of money available for this expense category for the month of August. This same procedure is used for each expense category. For example, the budgeted amount for Household remains at $30. But the actual expense for July was $38.00, which is $8 over the budget. This amount is written in the "Overage (Under)" column. Since the July expense was $8 over budget, this amount is subtracted from the $30 budgeted amount ($30 - $8 = $22), and $22 is written in the "Available This Month" column.

Table 11 shows the completed budget sheet for August at the end of the month. There were some expenses which exceeded the "Available This Month" amounts and some expenses less than that. Again, this is normal. For example, car expenses were high because tires were purchased for both Norman and Cathy's cars. Although this was an anticipated expense in Norman and Cathy's budget, it does not happen every month, or even every year. This will average out fine in future months.

TABLE 10

MONTHLY BUDGET EXPENSE FORM

MONTH __August__

	Budget	Overage (Under)	Available This Mo.
CARS – MAINT – REPAIRS	$270	($245)	$515
Sum for Month $			
HOUSEHOLD	$30	$8	$22
Sum for Month $			
MEDICAL	$145	($75)	$220
Sum for Month $			
UTILITIES	$250	($178)	$428
Sum for Month $			

TABLE 11

MONTHLY BUDGET EXPENSE FORM

MONTH __August__

	Budget	Overage (Under)	Available This Mo.
CARS – MAINT – REPAIRS	$270	($245)	$515
Norman's Car: Lube & Oil Change: $25, Tires: $380			
Cathy's Car: Tires: $300			
Sum for Month $705.00			
HOUSEHOLD	$30	$8	$22
Fuel for Gas Grill: $7			
Gas for Mower: $3			
Sum for Month $10.00			
MEDICAL	$145	($75)	$220
Norman: Dentist $100			
Children: Dentist: $100			
Sum for Month $200.00			
UTILITIES	$250	($178)	$428
Gas Bill: $7			
Electric Bill: $65			
Water & Sewage Bill: $40			
Sum for Month $112.00			

Table 12 is the budget sheet for the month of September. The amounts written in the "Overage (Under)" and "Available This Month" columns were calculated in the same manner as shown previously. For example, the expenses for cars was $705 in August. Since $515 was available, the expense was over by ($705 - $515) = $190. Hence, $190 is written in the "Overage (Under)" column. Since the expense was over budget, the $190 is subtracted from the $270 budget monthly amount ($270 - $190 = $80), and $80 is written in the "Available This Month" column. Similarly, the $10 household expenses was under the $22 available in August by $12. So ($12) is written in the "Overage (Under) column. Since this expense was under budget by $12, this amount is added to the $30 budgeted monthly amount (which is $42), and $42 is written in the "Available This Month" column. Then the expenses in September are written on this sheet as was done in the previous months.

Implementing this procedure is far easier than reading about it. Try it and you will see. And it will be very effective in helping you stay within your financial plan so you can achieve your long term goals.

If you find that one of the expenses is exceeding the budget by a large amount month after month after month, or another expense is less than budget by a large amount month after month after month, look very closely at the expenses for these items. If the monies spent for these budgeted expenses are all reasonable, it may be wise to adjust your budget to the actual expenses you are experiencing. On the other hand, if you find monies are being spent on things that were not planned for, or not needed, or frivolous things, you will have a choice to make. Either discontinue the expenditures on the non-planned items, not needed or frivolous things, or adjust your budget to allow for them. It is not a question of what is the right or wrong thing to do. It is a personal choice for you and your family to make.

TABLE 12

MONTHLY BUDGET EXPENSE FORM

MONTH September

	Budget	Overage (Under)	Available This Mo.
CARS – MAINT – REPAIRS	$270	$190	$80
Sum for Month $			
HOUSEHOLD	$30	($12)	$42
Sum for Month $			
MEDICAL	$145	($20)	$165
Sum for Month $			
UTILITIES	$250	($316)	$566
Sum for Month $			

TABLE 13

SAVINGS FOR ANTICIPATED FUTURE EXPENSES

Expense   Date of Deposit

	1/5	1/12	1/19	1/26	2/2	2/9	2/16	2/23	3/2	3/9	3/16	3/23	3/30	4/6	4/13	4/20	4/27	5/4	5/11	5/16	5/23	5/30	6/6	6/13	6/20	6/27
Medical																										
College																										
Vacation																										
Retirement																										
Down Pymnt on new house																										
Other																										
Total Deposit																										

5. The total for the anticipated future expenses for which you are now saving toward monthly (Item 4 of Table 7) should be divided by 4.33 (the number of weeks in a month). Each week, write a check for this amount and deposit it into a special separate account for these anticipated future expenses. Table 13 shows a method of keeping track of your deposits for the anticipated future expenses for the first six months of the year. A similar table would be required for the last half of the year with appropriate date changes. Each week you make a deposit, write in the total amount deposited for that week, as well as the amount for each anticipated expense. The date of your deposits, of course, may be different than those shown in the Table 13 example.

Since these anticipated expenses are all expected to occur sixty days or more in the future (for some anticipated expenses, perhaps years from now), the account for these anticipated expenses should be the type of account which will earn money for you. You may want to consider a Certificate of Deposit, or perhaps invest a portion of it into stocks. A savings account is *not* recommended since the interest earned typically will be very low. A good financial advisor[6] can guide you on this.

---

[6] *Your accountant may be able to provide you guidance. If not, he, or your attorney, may be able to recommend a good financial advisor. You may want to consider a relatively small financial institution. My experience with a large financial institution, such as Merrill Lynch, has been that following their investment advice resulted in small profits or losses.*

CHAPTER 4

STEPS TO PURCHASING YOUR HOUSE

Having completed Chapters 2 and 3, and finding it would be wise for you to own your own house, the next questions to ponder are these:

1. Do I want to purchase an existing house that is not new?

2. Do I want to purchase a new existing house?

3. Do I want to build a new house?

There is no magic right answer. It all depends on your goals and desires. This chapter will discuss the purchasing of a new existing house or purchasing an existing house that is not new. See Chapter 5 if you would like to build a new house.

The first step is to select an attorney. Don't be fooled by a mortgage company or a realtor that may say you don't need an attorney since you will be paying for an attorney at closing. While there will be an attorney at the closing, and part of your closing expenses will be for that attorney's fees, that attorney will be working to protect the mortgage company – not you. And his duties will essentially be that of a clerk, making sure all papers are there properly signed and notarized, and all appropriate parties paid. You will need to hire your own attorney to look out for your interests.

I have personally used the services of seventeen attorneys. Only three of them have provided services that I would consider as competent and honest. Consequently, I believe you will find it challenging to find a good, experienced real estate attorney to represent you.

From my experience, the best way to find a good attorney is to ask friends you know well for their recommendations *based on their personal experiences.* A recommendation based upon what someone has heard about an attorney is virtually worthless. Your church and the Better Business Bureau in your community may also be able to provide recommendations on good attorneys, and attorneys to avoid. It would also be wise to interview the attorney you plan on choosing to assure you can work comfortably with them. Ask your attorney for a written estimate of what they will do and what their fees will be for this service. And above all, make sure your attorney of choice is highly experienced with real estate transactions.

My experience has shown that one of the most useless ways of finding a good attorney is to ask the local bar association. When asked for a recommendation, bar associations typically sound like they are reading from a list of contributors to the bar – or reading from the yellow pages in the telephone book – and when pressed for a specific recommendation (good or bad), they refused to do so.

The second step is to select a buyer's realtor – and to list realtors that should be avoided. If you contact realtors who advertise houses for sale, you will be contacting *seller's realtors.* They represent the seller. They do their best to sell houses at the highest price possible. After all, their income is a percentage of the selling price. And since they represent the seller, they may be reluctant to disclose disadvantages of the seller's house. Your interests will be best served with a *buyer's realtor.* This is a realtor who will work for *you* and do their best to find a house that meets your budget and your desires, while also looking for any disadvantages that exist in houses. They can also recommend mortgage companies that should be considered, and those that should be avoided. You will need to pay this realtor a fee, or they may agree to accept a percentage of the price you pay for your house. Your attorney may be able to recommend a buyer's realtor. Your friends, church, and the Better Business Bureau may also be able to provide input from their personal experiences.

The third step is to prepare financially to purchase your house. You have already prepared yourself financially to purchase your house by preparing a budget, getting your debt minimized, cleaning up any credit problems, and saving money in order to provide a 20% down payment and have ample cash to pay for closing costs and a cash reserve. Now you need to put your achievements to work for you.

The first step is to order a current credit report (unless you have recently done so, as suggested on Page 1). In fact, this should be the very first step taken when you are ready to purchase your house, even before selecting an attorney. When you receive the report, review it carefully with your buyer's realtor. There should be nothing derogatory in the report. If there is anything derogatory, find out why, and take action to correct it immediately. Likewise, if there are any errors, or some of your credit history is omitted, get them corrected immediately. You want to have all of your credit history included, showing you are a person who pays your bills in full and on time. Your buyer's realtor and, if necessary, your attorney, can help you with this.

Order another credit report two months after making any corrections to your credit report. Check it carefully to assure anything derogatory has been removed, and any errors or omissions have been corrected.

After you have received a good credit report with no errors or omissions and nothing derogatory, contact three appropriate mortgage companies and ask for "pre-qualification" for a mortgage. Basically, they will ask you for the information that is in Table 2. Your buyer's realtor can help you with this, and can also recommend mortgage companies to contact. The mortgage companies will respond with a letter which will state, in essence, that you are "pre-qualified" for a mortgage of a certain dollar amount at a certain interest rate, based upon the information you have provided them. Review the letters of "pre-qualification" with your buyer's realtor. Select the best one to be your mortgage company. Then ask that mortgage company for *pre-approval* of a mortgage.

"Pre-qualification" and "pre-approval" are very different and must not be confused. "Pre-qualification" is a very casual process where the mortgage company essentially says you can *probably* obtain a mortgage of a certain amount at a certain interest rate *based upon the information you have told them*. "Pre-approval", by contrast, is much more rigorous and includes providing the mortgage company with many documents, such as income tax returns, pay check stubs, etc. It is actually applying for a mortgage. When you get your "pre-approval" notification from the mortgage company, it will be their *commitment* to provide you with a mortgage of a certain amount and at a certain interest rate.

Sellers put very little stock in "pre-qualification" letters. When you receive "pre-approval" from a mortgage company, though, it is like you are holding cash in your hand to purchase a house. Sellers and seller's realtors will be very, very interested in you, and will be much more willing to negotiate on the selling price and fees.

The fourth step is to choose a licensed house inspector. This will be an expert on house construction and maintenance who will be able to closely examine the house you want to purchase and discover any defects. He will present a written report of his findings to you.

Again, your friends may be able to provide recommendations based upon their personal experiences. The Better Business Bureau in your community, your attorney, realtor, and your church may also be able to provide guidance.

The fifth step is to select a house appraiser. An appraiser will look at the house you have decided to purchase and determine what a fair price would be on the open market.

You may wonder why you should hire your own appraiser when the mortgage company will have an appraiser evaluate the house before agreeing to provide you a mortgage, and that appraiser's fee will be part of your closing costs. The answer is the mortgage company's appraiser is looking out for the interests of the mortgage company and, perhaps, the seller. They will *not* be looking out for your interests. Hence, they will want to appraise a house at a price that is as high as possible.

An appraiser is supposed to value a house by looking at its size, type of structure (brick, vinyl siding, one or two story, basement or slab construction, etc.), internal features, lot size, etc., and compare it with very similar houses in the neighborhood that have recently been sold. It is quite subjective, depending heavily on the skill, judgment, and integrity of the appraiser, at best. Some appraisers have been known to sit in their car and look at a house from the street and "determine" the value of a house without ever setting foot in the house or taking any measurements.

Mortgage companies want to sell the largest mortgages possible to maximize their profits. And sellers want to sell their houses at the highest possible price. So an appraiser working for a mortgage company or seller will be under pressure to appraise a house at the highest possible price. This appraiser may well compare your house to other houses in the general area that he knows were sold well above their fair market price. The result will be the house you have chosen will be appraised above the fair open market price.

If you think this doesn't happen, you may want to talk with Mr. Francisca Noya[7]. He bought a home in the Poconos of Pennsylvania for $159,000, the appraised price, in 1999. When he tried to sell it a year later, it would only bring $85,000. His case was not an isolated case. There were more than 600 families sucked in by this scam by builders, appraisers and mortgage companies in the Poconos. Similarly, seven appraisers in Minnesota recently lost their licenses for inflating property appraisals. Why do appraisers do this? At least two appraisers in the Poconos stated they had been pressured by builders and mortgage companies to inflate appraisals. When one of them balked, they were threatened, and told they would not get any more work.

Though it may cost an extra few hundred dollars, hiring your own appraiser could save you thousands of dollars in the cost of a house. Your realtor, house inspector and attorney may be able to recommend a good appraiser who is not connected to the seller or a mortgage company. On the other hand, if your realtor is highly skilled and experienced in doing CMA's (comparative market analysis, which is essentially determining the fair market value of a house by comparing it to similar houses which have recently been sold), your realtor may be able to provide you the fair open market price for the house of your choice, eliminating the need of hiring an appraiser.

The sixth step is to let your buyer's realtor, attorney, appraiser and house inspector do their jobs. Listen to what they say. They are working for you and trying to get the best house possible for you at minimum cost. Your realtor and appraiser may recommend _not_ purchasing a house that you have fallen in love with because of excessive price, location, etc. – things they would be familiar with due to experience. Consult with your attorney and realtor before making an offer. Make sure the offer contains a clause which gives you the

---

[7] *Not his true name.*

right to withdraw your offer if defects are found by your house inspector or you are not able to get financing for the house for any reason. *Do not sign any paper or make any agreement with anyone without consulting with your attorney, realtor, and house inspector in advance, as appropriate.* Though you may be pressured to sign papers or act quickly without an opportunity to consult with your people, *this pressure must be resisted.* I say this from personal experience. See Biography in the Appendix.

If your attorney, realtor or house inspector find problems with the house or purchase agreement, listen to what they say. Follow their advice. They are approaching the house purchase objectively from an investment standpoint with your best interests at heart. If you are a typical house buyer, you will see things through rose colored glasses and not see many of the defects that exist (which is what the seller's realtor and house seller want). Some house defects may be minor, and repairs negotiable with the seller. Others may be very serious, and require repair by the seller, or make the house unsuitable to purchase. Make sure these problems have been corrected, and your house inspector confirms they have been properly corrected, *before* you agree to purchase the house.

The seller might promise to have the defects repaired after you purchase the house. Be wary of such promises. Once you have purchased the house, and the seller has been paid and moved away, it may be very difficult (or impossible) to force the seller to make the promised repairs. It is much better to have any repairs *completed, inspected and approved by your house inspector before purchasing the house.* It is possible this will delay your purchasing the house and moving in. Consequently, it is wise to plan in advance to live in your present home for an additional few weeks until all defects are corrected.

The seventh step is to close on your house purchase. The mortgage company will prepare closing papers, which are the legal papers stating you have purchased your house, lists all charges for doing so, and that you agree to pay the company a certain total dollar amount and certain monthly payments. _THE CLOSING PAPERS MUST BE PRESENTED TO YOU AND YOUR ATTORNEY FOR YOUR REVIEW AND APPROVAL AT LEAST A WEEK PRIOR TO THE SCHEDULED CLOSING. IF THE MORTGAGE COMPANY WILL NOT DO THIS, WALK AWAY FROM THAT COMPANY – THEY ARE PROBABLY TRYING TO SCREW YOU._ In fact, it is law in many states that a mortgage company must present closing papers to a buyer a week prior to closing. Review the papers carefully with your attorney and realtor. Ask questions on anything you do not understand. There is no such thing as a dumb question – only dummies who don't ask questions. When you sign the closing papers, you will be making perhaps the most expensive purchase in your life. If there are any errors or anything that you, your attorney or realtor do not agree with, ask your attorney to get the papers corrected _immediately –well before the closing._ Of course, do not sign any documents until you, your attorney and your realtor agree the documents are proper, and you understand all documents. And do not move into the house or take possession of it until after the closing.

Having followed the procedures outlined in Chapters 2, 3, and this chapter, you will have purchased a structurally sound house which best meets your goals and expectations with the best financial agreement possible, and with a sound financial budget. You will have an opportunity to enjoy your home for many years with minimum risk of financial hardship.

CHAPTER 5

STEPS TO BUILDING YOUR HOUSE

Designing your house so that it is exactly as you want it and then watching it be built can be a wonderful experience. If this is what you would like to do, you will need to do several things:

1. Plan on spending two years from the beginning of planning your house until you move in.

2. Plan on spending more money for the house than if you purchased an existing house.

3. Plan on spending a lot of time planning your house, selecting materials for the house, meeting or talking with your house inspector *daily*, and visiting your house during construction from time to time. Your house inspector will be inspecting the construction of the house virtually daily.

4. Plan on spending at least two months in your present location after your new house is scheduled to be completed. In spite of meticulous planning, overseeing construction, and the best efforts of an excellent general contractor, there will almost always be a delay in completion due to material shortages, subcontractor problems, and bad weather. In addition, the completed house will almost always contain some defects or deviations from what you specified. These need to be corrected *before* you move in or accept the house.

5. Have infinite patience. Even if you are fortunate enough to get a general contractor who is impeccably honest, highly skilled and with extensive experience, there can be honest misunderstandings between you and them. In addition, the general contractor will probably hire many subcontractors to do specialized jobs (such as masons for concrete and brick work, electricians for electrical work, plumbers for plumbing

work, etc.). The general contractor must tell each subcontractor _exactly_ what you want. If a subcontractor does not fully understand exactly what you want, it is virtually a certainty they will do something that is not in agreement with what you want. And even if the subcontractor fully understands what you want, there is a good chance they will have an employee who either is not well skilled in his job, has a bad day, or really doesn't care about the quality of his work, resulting in defects and deviations from what you want.

A house is a very complex structure. Taking shortcuts will likely result in a house with defects – some of which may not show up for years. In addition, short-cutting the above steps is likely to result in a lot of frustration for you and confrontations with construction personnel, and your house not being built exactly as you want. If you do not have the time and patience to do all of the above, it is strongly recommended that you not build your house.

If you have the time, patience, money, and desire to design and build your house, then proceed as shown below, and _relax and enjoy the experience._

1. Build Your Team (approximately a three month process)

You are about to undertake the construction of a house on which you will be paying for the next thirty years. It needs to be located on property that meets your needs, and that you will be happy with for many years. The house needs to be what _you_ want. It must be structurally sound. It must meet building codes. The purchase agreement must be written to provide you with a quality house and protection in case of construction errors. And the mortgage needs to provide you the most economical means available for purchasing the house.

Building your team is the most important step in your journey. It must be done thoughtfully and carefully for your house to meet your expectations and to minimize expenses. The team members you select must not only be knowledgeable and reputable, but all must be able to work well together and with you. Each team member should also be independent from other team members to avoid any chance of conflict of interest. For example, avoid a realtor who has land for sale, or works for a builder. They may not have your best interests at heart. And using an architect who is the brother of your builder or an employee of your builder is not a good practice. They may work in the best interests of the builder – not you.

Select an attorney. Don't be fooled by anyone who tells you that you don't need to hire an attorney since there will be a closing attorney at the loan closing. While there will be an attorney at the closing, and part of your closing expenses will be for that attorney's fees, that attorney will be working to protect the mortgage company – not you. And his duties will essentially be that of a clerk, making sure all papers are there, properly signed and notarized, and all appropriate parties paid. You will need to hire your own attorney to look out for your interests. From my experience, the best way to find a good attorney is to ask friends you know well for their recommendations *based on their personal experiences – not what they have heard about an attorney.* The local Better Business Bureau and your church may also be able to assist you on this. It would also be wise to interview prospective attorneys to see with whom you are most comfortable working. Ask them to specify in writing exactly what they will be doing for you and their estimated fees. Also, the attorney must have extensive experience in real estate. Calling a bar association is not recommended. My experience is they are about as useless as using the yellow pages of the telephone book.

Select a buyer's realtor. The primary responsibility of the realtor will be to assist you in finding property that will be suitable for your new house; that meets your requirements on location, terrain, etc.; and that is priced as low as possible.

They can also do a "CMA" (Comparative Market Analysis) to determine what the market value will be for your new house.[8] Discuss the realtor's role with them, and ask them for a written fee agreement. Though the realtor should be consulted as you develop your house plans, the role of the realtor will be much less than when you are looking for a house that has already been built. However, the realtor will be your key to avoiding a lot that is in a poor location with respect to crime, schools, anticipated future growth in the area, etc., and to avoiding price gouging by a greedy builder. Your attorney, co-workers, friends, church, and Better Business Bureau may be able to refer you to a good realtor based upon their personal experiences.

Select an architect. The architect will be responsible for designing the house exactly as you want, and also comply with building codes, and provide you with a safe, durable house. If there is something you have requested that should not be done or would be unreasonably expensive to do, it is his/her responsibility to bring this to your attention; explain why; and propose an alternative. The architect MUST be very detailed in the drawings made for your house. Nothing can be left open to question or interpretation by the general contractor or a subcontractor. If anything is left undefined or vague, it is very likely the house will not be built exactly as you want. If you have questions or you feel something is not well defined or correct on the drawings, ask questions. Naturally, your architect should specify in writing exactly what he/she will be doing for you; estimate when their work will begin and be completed; and provide an estimate of their fees.

---

[8] *This will be a valuable tool to determine if the price quotations provided by builders to build your house are reasonable. Though your custom built house may cost more than standard houses that are already built, it should not be vastly more expensive. Your realtor and architect can help you to determine if the quotations from builders are reasonably in line with the market value of the house as determined by the realtor.*

A house built in Oak Creek, Wisconsin is an example of what can happen. A young couple built their first new house – without hiring their own architect or house inspector. They requested the front of the house near the entry door be constructed of brick. What they wanted was brick everywhere near the entry door. What they got is shown in Figure 1 (street view of the house), which appears to be what they wanted. The recess around the front door was not brick, though, as shown in Figure 2. Similarly, the joint between the garage walls and the floor was not trimmed with molding or sealed (see Figure 3). In addition to being unsightly, the gap allowed mice and insects to enter the house from the garage. Surprisingly, the gap between the garage walls and floor was considered acceptable by the city building inspector. Careful, detailed work by your architect will prevent errors like this.

Your realtor, attorney and friends may be able to recommend an architect based upon their personal experiences. The Better Business Bureau in your community and your church may also be able to provide guidance. Again, a personal interview would be wise to assure you will be able to comfortably work with the architect of your choice.

Figure 1

Figure 2

Figure 3

Select a licensed house inspector. Your licensed house inspector will be an expert on house construction and construction procedures. They will inspect the construction of your house on a daily basis to assure construction is in accordance with the architect's drawings, in compliance with building codes, and in compliance with good construction practices. Your realtor, attorney, architect, church, friends, and Better Business Bureau may be able to recommend a good inspector. It is no accident that your builder was not recommended as a source for references for a house inspector. A builder might recommend a house inspector that is very easy to work with and will allow inferior materials or workmanship.

It would also be wise to personally interview the house inspector you are considering as your choice. You will need to feel comfortable in placing great trust in your inspector. They will be the person inspecting your house and representing you in meetings with the builder, and who will authorize paying your loan money to the general contractor for work performed during construction. You also need to know you can work and communicate well with them since you will be working with them on almost a daily basis for perhaps a year. Naturally, the house inspector should provide in writing exactly what he/she will be doing for you, and an estimate of their fees.

Select suitable general contractors (at least two). Your attorney, architect, house inspector, realtor, friends and church may be able to provide recommendations. The Better Business Bureau may be able to tell you the names of general contractors for whom they have received complaints (builders you should avoid), but may not be able to recommend a good general contractor. Personally interview general contractors to assure you and your house inspector can communicate and work well with the ones of your choice. Tell them in general terms the type of house you plan to build (e.g., ranch type, brick, approximate square feet, slab or basement, etc.). Make sure they are comfortable with and experienced in building the type of house you want. Ask where they have built similar houses. Then go see those houses and talk with the owners, asking of their experiences with their house and the general contractors. Ask specifically if there were any problems. And ask them if they know of any other houses the general contractors have built. This may open the door to your learning of other houses the general contractors have built which they did not tell you about because of problems.

Discuss any problems found in the houses previously built by the general contractors with your architect and house inspector. Then have a meeting with your architect, house inspector, and each general contractor you are considering. Discuss the problems found in houses built by each general contractor and ask for their solutions. If the responses of a general contractor are not satisfactory with you, your architect and house inspector, you will probably want to eliminate that general contractor.

It would be wise to select at least two general contractors who you feel satisfy your requirements. After your house is designed by your architect, you will be asking the contractors for quotations on building your house. You will want at least two quotations.

Table 1 shows the expenses that would be incurred in purchasing an *existing* $180,000 house. When you design and build a new house, your attorney and house inspector will be required to perform much more work than if you purchased an existing house. Hence, their expenses will be more than shown in Table 1. You will also need the services of an architect, which was not required to purchase an existing house. The total expenses for the services of these professional people can vary greatly, from perhaps $2,000 to more than $5,000, depending upon the complexity of your house and the services required from them. Whatever they estimate their total cost will be, plan on the cost being double the estimated cost. Also, have these funds available before *any* work is done by your team. For example, if they respond that their estimated total cost will be $4,000, plan on having at least $8,000 immediately available to pay for their services. Planning and constructing a house have a way of becoming more time consuming than planned – and the expenses of these professional people are based upon the hours they work for you. Perhaps their expenses will not be double their estimate. But it is better to anticipate a high cost and be prepared for it than to be unable to pay the costs when the estimates are exceeded.

2. Select Your Mortgage Company

You have already prepared yourself financially for building your house by preparing a budget; getting your debt minimized; cleaning up any credit problems; making sure your credit report is accurate and very favorable; saving in order to provide a 20% down payment; having ample cash to pay for closing costs; and having a cash reserve. Now you need to put your achievements to work for you.

Contact three appropriate mortgage companies and ask for "pre-qualification" for a mortgage. Basically, they will ask you for the information that is in Table 2. Your realtor can help you with this, and can also recommend mortgage companies to contact. The mortgage companies will respond with a letter which will state, in essence, that you are "pre-qualified" for a mortgage of a certain dollar amount at a certain interest rate, based upon the information you have provided them. Review the letters of "pre-qualification" with your realtor. Select the best one to be your mortgage company. Then ask that mortgage company for _pre-approval_ of a mortgage. Pre-approval is actually a commitment by a mortgage company to provide you a mortgage of a certain dollar amount at a certain interest rate. To obtain this, you will need to apply for a mortgage. Your realtor or attorney can help you with this. Be sure your mortgage includes provision for a lot.

3. Design Your House; Select Your Lot; Select Your General Contractor (six to nine months)

The length of time for this step may be more or less than shown, depending upon the workload of your team, the complexity of your house, and how much time is required to find a suitable lot.

Before starting to design your house or selecting your lot, read Chapter 6, House Design Considerations, and Chapter 7, Safety And Security. These chapters present factors that should be considered as you design your house, but which are often overlooked. While working with your architect on the house design, be sure to bring your house inspector and realtor in to review your final house design. They will have a lot of practical experience with houses and may see a potential problem. It would be wise to get their opinions. After there is a "meeting of the minds" on the design of the house, present it to the general contractors for their review. They may also recommend some changes – which should be reviewed by you, your architect and house inspector. Upon agreement of the house plans by you, your architect and house inspector, ask for quotations from at least two general contractors that you consider to be the best.

You will need to select your lot before your house design is completed. The size, shape and topography of your lot (i.e., is it hilly; fill dirt needed; lots of large rocks; etc.) will determine if the lot of your choice is suitable for your house. Your architect, house inspector, general contractors, and realtor can inform you of available lots. If the lot of your choice is not suitable, you may need to select another lot, or modify the design of your house. Take your architect, house inspector and general contractors to the lot of your choice to make sure it is compatible with your planned house. Your general contractors will also need this information in order to provide accurate quotations.

Select your general contractor based upon their reputation for honesty, quality and reliability, as well as the price quotation – with priority given to the first three qualities. Have your attorney draft an agreement. It is strongly recommended that a "warranty bond" of at least 10% of the value of the house be provided in the agreement for a period of at least two years. The general contractor may object to this – and for this reason, and in order to get an accurate cost for the bond, it should not be brought up until after the quotation is received. However, you should have this tool to assure any house defects will be corrected at no cost to you, even if the general contractor goes out of business. If the general contractor retires or goes out of business after building your house, you may not be able to look to them for warranty repairs. Of course, there will be some expense for a "warranty bond", but it should not be more than a few hundred dollars.

Be careful to avoid "house warranty" programs that many contractors like to offer house buyers. These warranties typically have two major "flaws": (1) The *builder* is the warrantor for the first one or two years; (2) If there is any controversy or claim or complaint, <u>it must be settled by binding arbitration with an arbitrator; you give up your right to file a law suit in court.</u>. If the builder's company ceases to exist after building your house, you may have no one to turn to with a warranty claim for the first year or two – or possibly forever. I have personally experienced having a new house with defects and a house warranty where binding arbitration was required. It turned out the arbitrator was another builder – and though he could see cracked walls, water damage from a leaking roof, and a well that would run out of water in our one year old house in Fayetteville, Georgia, the arbitrator ruled <u>*in favor of the builder, stating he was not liable for the repair of any defects*</u> (See Biography in the Appendix for details).

Your general contractor will want to be paid periodically during the construction period. Typically, the mortgage company will establish a "construction loan" for you, which will provide for payments to the general contractor as construction milestones are achieved. Your general contractor may want to set up a "draw" with the mortgage company which will allow *them* to go directly to the mortgage company and draw money *on your loan* periodically *based upon the milestones they tell the mortgage company have been completed.* Providing draw payments for work completed is fine. But giving the general contractor authorization to draw on your loan is giving them a blank check. And the mortgage company may not know – or care – if the draw request is legitimate, for the more money they can loan to you for a longer period of time, the more interest they can charge you. Your house inspector should be the only party authorized to approve draws on your construction loan. This will force the general contractor to go to your house inspector and state that certain construction milestones have been achieved and request a draw. Your house inspector will know if the milestones have been achieved and if the work was done properly. If the milestones were not reached, or the construction work is inferior – no draw payment. Your general contractor will know this, and will be discouraged from doing inferior work or attempting unwarranted draws.

Upon completion of your house, the construction loan will be rolled into your final mortgage.

4. Build Your House (approximately nine months)

After working about nine months to a year, you will have selected your attorney, realtor, house inspector, architect, general contractor, and mortgage company. You will have selected and purchased your lot; completed your house design; and have agreements with your mortgage company to pay for the construction of the house and your long term mortgage. You will have a contract with your general contractor, and are now ready to start construction of your house.

The ball is now in the court of your general contractor. He will need to obtain the appropriate building permits; contract with subcontractors; obtain materials; and last but not least, contend with the weather.

Your contract with the general contractor will typically require you to select appliances, light fixtures, carpeting, floor vinyl, plumbing fixtures, etc. for your house from lists of vendors, and will allow certain dollar amounts for each item. You will need to act promptly on this so that your general contractor can order the appropriate materials and have them on hand when needed. Incidentally, you do not need to limit yourself to the list of vendors that the general contractor may provide. If you want certain materials from another supplier, consult with your house inspector. Just keep in mind that time is critical. Act promptly. If you want some special item from a supplier that is not on the general contractor's list and it will require eight weeks to get that item – and the general contractor will need it in four weeks to install – you have a problem. Specifying that item and supplier could delay construction of your house by four weeks or more.

As you observe your house being constructed, you may have questions about certain things. <u>*Do not raise your questions with the general contractor or subcontractors.*</u> Present them to your house inspector. The general contractor needs to hear from one person – your inspector – to avoid confusion and minimize misunderstandings. Your inspector will be inspecting the construction of your house regularly and will be able to answer your questions. Likewise, any questions the general contractor or a subcontractor may ask you, or any papers they may present to you for your signature, should be referred to your inspector, and perhaps to your attorney if appropriate. What may appear to be an innocent question or document requiring your signature may actually be an effort to circumvent part of your contract with the contractor so they can build your house with less cost – and less quality.

Once construction has started, try to avoid making any design changes to your house. What may appear to be a simple design change may require additional architectural work, new permits, new materials, new subcontractors, etc. It almost assures a cost increase and perhaps a delay in completion of your house. If there is something that you urgently want to change, though, discuss it with your architect and house inspector as soon as possible. They will work with you to try to achieve the changes you desire with minimum cost and construction delay.

Plan on your house being completed no sooner than two months after your general contractor projects it will be ready for you. Hence, if he/she says it will take nine months to build your house, plan on it requiring eleven months. Adverse weather, delays in obtaining materials, and delays in work by subcontractors will invariably push the completion date past the expected completion date. And once the house is completed, a close inspection by you and your house inspector together will reveal defects or deviations from your specifications. These should be reported to the general contractor by your house inspector and corrected _before_ you accept or move into your house.

Before accepting or moving into your house, the mortgage company should provide you with loan closing papers. Review them carefully with your attorney to assure that you fully understand them, and they are acceptable. If you do not understand something, ask questions. _Do not accept or move into the new house until you and your attorney have reviewed the closing papers; found them to be acceptable; and closed the purchase of the house._

Designing and building a new house that meets your dreams is something most people do not have an opportunity to do. And many who build their new houses find what should be a joyful time turn into a nightmare. If you have done your homework thoroughly in the financial analyses (Chapters 2 and 3) and in preparing to build your home (as presented in this chapter), though, chances are very good your house will be exactly as you want it. *Take time to enjoy watching your new home constructed. This is a joy that only a few people have an opportunity to enjoy.*

CHAPTER 6

HOUSE DESIGN CONSIDERATIONS

The purpose of this chapter is to present the advantages and disadvantages of certain design features in a house. Since many of the features can be incorporated into an existing house as well as a new house that is being designed, this chapter is applicable to everyone who is planning to purchase a house or currently owns a house. It is suggested that you visit houses with the various features presented and ask the owners for their experiences. Your architect, house inspector or realtor may be able to help you find houses with these design features.

This chapter will enable you to make your house even more enjoyable and less costly to own in future years. The features are presented in alphabetical order.

Air Quality Control

The materials used in modern houses contain many chemicals, some of which produce fumes and tiny particles for a long time after installation. With the improved sealing of doors, windows and walls in newer houses, these contaminants – some of which are toxic – build up in the house, causing the air inside the house to be much more toxic than the air outdoors, often causing the occupants to suffer a variety of ailments. These impurities need to be removed.

A two step process is recommended to accomplish this. First, a good filtration system should be installed on the furnace/air conditioning system. The filter typically provided with a furnace/air conditioner system does not provide the fine filtration needed to remove these tiny particles, and does nothing to remove any gases. A "HEPA" (high efficiency particulate air) filter or an electrostatic filter should be installed. It can be an integral part of your furnace/air conditioning system. Your architect, house inspector, general contractor or an experienced heating/air conditioning specialist can provide detailed information on systems that are best suited for your house.

The "HEPA" or electronic filter will remove particulate impurities from the air, including dust, pollens and molds. But they will not remove the gaseous fumes of the materials from the air. Hence, the second step is to install a fresh air ventilation system. This would simply be a small blower that will bring fresh air into the furnace/air conditioning system immediately before the "HEPA" or electrostatic filter system, thereby filtering out any particulate impurities in the incoming air. The blower would be connected such that it operated whenever the blower for the furnace/air conditioner system was operating. See Figure 4 for a schematic of this system. The vents for your kitchen range and the bathrooms will provide a means for the stale air to be exhausted from your house.

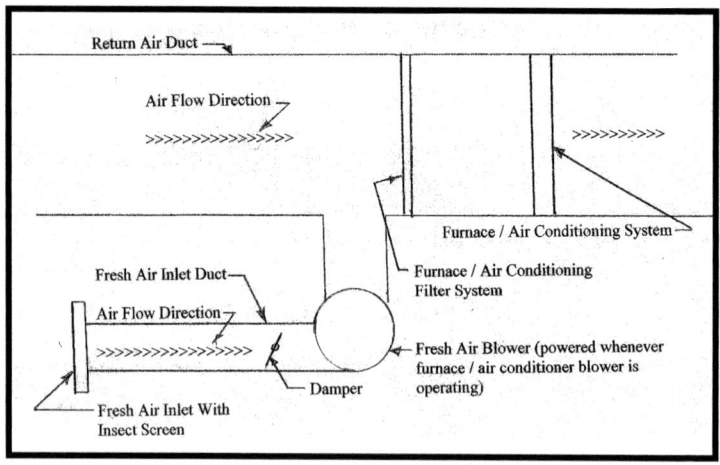

Figure 4
Fresh Air Ventilation System Schematic

The amount of fresh air needed in a house daily will depend upon the size of the house, the amount of gaseous contamination generated by the materials in the house, the number of people in the house, the amount of smoking in the house, etc. Translation: There is no exact answer. It is suggested that a centrifugal type blower be used which has an air flow capacity (in cubic feet per minute) of 3% times the square feet of the house. Hence, a house with 1,800 square feet would be equipped with a fresh air blower with a capacity of (3% x 1,800) or 54 cubic feet per minute. Though this may have the capacity to produce more fresh air than is needed, the fresh air brought into the house can be reduced by the damper.

Finally, there is one other air "contaminant" that needs to be controlled. Moisture (or humidity) is always present in air, and is needed *at a reasonable level (40% to 50%)* to prevent respiratory discomfort, condensation, and the formation of mold. People breathing, perspiring, showering, bathing and cooking all add moisture to the air. If moisture is continually added to the air and none is removed, the relative humidity will continue to increase to an extremely high level. The house will feel uncomfortable; people will perspire easily; and moisture will condense on cooler surfaces (such as windows in the winter and in closets), allowing mold to form. Some forms of mold will cause illness, or death, to people, and must be prevented.

The fresh air ventilation system will help control excessive humidity. The air conditioning system will also help control humidity in the summer months. These often provide adequate humidity control. If you find your home has high humidity (over 55%), or moisture condensing on cold windows or tile floors in the winter, though, a dehumidifier may also be needed. Installation of a dehumidifier will remove excessive moisture from the air. Your architect or house inspector can provide detailed guidance for you.

Basement, Slab or Crawl Space House?

A house built on a slab of concrete is the most economical house to build and can be constructed in the least amount of time. Typical practice is to install heating ducts and water pipes in the concrete slab. There are disadvantages, though, including: (1) cold floors, especially vinyl or tile floors, in winter months; (2) possibility of moisture forming on vinyl floors in winter months, making them slippery as well as cold, and possibly causing mold to form; (3) rooms located furthest from the furnace will be colder than other rooms in winter months due to duct cooling by the concrete slab (perhaps as much as 10 degrees colder than rooms nearest the furnace); (4) hot water supplied to rooms furthest from the water heater will be substantially cooler than for nearby rooms (perhaps as much as 15 degrees cooler), and the hot water tap will need to run for some time before hot water is flowing from the tap, resulting in slightly higher utility bills; (5) deterioration of a pipe in the slab due to corrosion, or a crack forming in the slab and causing a water pipe to break, requiring part of the slab to be broken apart with a cement drill and the pipe replaced. Though this is not a frequent problem, it is a time-consuming, dirty, expensive repair (though insurance may provide some financial protection from this potential problem). If the lower cost and shorter construction time for a house built on a concrete slab offset these shortcomings for you, this type of house may meet your needs well. It is recommended, though, that the furnace/air conditioner be placed in the attic with the registers in the walls instead of the floor. This will prevent some rooms from being colder than other rooms in the winter. It will also eliminate the possibility of anything falling into registers, as can happen with floor registers. See Figure 5, for example, where a floor register is located one foot from the water closet in a new house. If the water closet should ever run over, it is obvious where the water will go.

(Note: If a gas furnace is used in the attic, be sure it has a pilot-less ignition system. You do not want to have the inconvenience of the pilot light in an attic furnace going out and requiring servicing).

A house with a basement is more expensive than a house built on a slab of concrete or with a crawl space. Typically, a basement will cost $19 to $22 per square foot – though, of course, it can vary considerably from this depending upon locality, type of soil, amount and size of any rocks or boulders that need to be removed, etc. Sometimes it is not possible to provide a basement due to excessive rocks and boulders and/or excessive moisture in the ground.

Figure 5
Floor Register Located Next To Water Closet In Slab House

Though a basement adds cost to a house, the cost is very low when looking at the overall cost of a house. A 2,000 square foot ranch house on a slab in Fort Wayne, Indiana, for example, cost $141,000. Adding a basement would have cost an additional $38,000 to $44,000. Heating and air conditioning expenses will not be changed materially, especially if the basement walls are finished.

A basement is an ideal place for the furnace, water heater, laundry facilities, work shop, storage, and for recreation. It is also an ideal place for protection from severe weather. And with a warm basement, the floors of the house will be warm in winter months, thereby feeling more comfortable and preventing the formation of moisture and mold.

A house with a crawl space is a compromise between a slab and a basement house. A crawl space typically provides two to three feet of space between the ground and the bottom of the ground floor of the house, enabling installation of the furnace, air conditioning, plumbing, and possibly water heater in this area. The crawl space needs to be ventilated to prevent a buildup of moisture. Consequently, care must be taken in winter months to limit the ventilation to prevent freezing of pipes.

For your safety, a house with a basement or crawl space should be checked for radon gas contamination. Radon is a colorless, odorless radioactive gas that comes out of the ground. It is the second largest cause of lung cancer, causing approximately 22,000 deaths each year. If radon gas is present, a ventilation system can be installed to remove the gas. Cost will normally be under $1,800.

Bathroom

A "bathroom", years ago, was an outhouse. As technology developed, it became a room inside the house. In recent years, it has become a sanctuary in many houses, including double showers, large jacuzzis, saunas, double sinks, etc. People today are spending $8,000 to $80,000 for a "bathroom". The specific design and features are left to the discretion of the reader.

Two features that can add considerable comfort in the bathroom are suggested for consideration. One is a radiant heater. Though a house may be comfortably warm for a clothed person, a person climbing out of a shower or bathtub will feel cold due to the water evaporating from their skin. Adding a heater that blows warm air in the bathroom is not a good solution, for the moving air causes moisture on the skin to evaporate more quickly, cooling a person even more. A radiant heater generates heat without causing air movement, thereby warming a person's moist skin comfortably and silently with no draft.

The second feature is a "point-of-use" water heater (sometimes called a "tank-less" water heater). The hot water taps in a bathroom located a distance from a conventional water heater may require running perhaps three gallons of water before warm water starts to flow from the tap due to the water in the pipe from the water heater being cooled by the air – or the cold concrete slab in the case of a slab house. After warm water begins to flow, it will continue to increase in temperature for a few minutes, making it necessary to continue to change the temperature setting of the water valve in order to maintain a comfortable water temperature. A "tank-less" water heater in each bathroom, kitchen, etc. eliminates these problems by instantly providing hot water at a constant temperature at each tap. "Tank-less" water heaters will cost more to install than one central water heater, but will reduce utility expenses since they will provide hot water more efficiently than the conventional tank type heater.

Ceiling Fans

In winter months, ceiling fans can effectively move warm air that has collected near the ceiling of a room down toward the floor, making the room temperature more even and comfortable. In the summer, ceiling fans enhance the performance of the house air conditioning system and make rooms feel more comfortable. In short, they make rooms more comfortable, summer and winter. They are recommended for bedrooms, living rooms and garden rooms. They are not recommended for the dining room or bathrooms.

Closets

Almost every house has insufficient closet space. Builders seem to avoid them as much as possible, perhaps because they cost money. It is much cheaper to place drywall over an area that is two feet wide and two feet deep than to frame it, install a door, drywall inside the area and paint it. But an area like this is ideal for a coat closet for guests, storage for the sweeper, Christmas decorations, children's toys, etc.

It is recommended that closets be installed wherever there is an area at least two feet wide and two feet deep. I have never seen a house that had "too much" closet space. Your architect can help you with this.

Electrical Generator

Generating electrical power at your house can be accomplished by either a fuel powered generator or a wind powered generator. Fuel powered generators create noise, exhaust fumes, and the total cost for the generator, its maintenance and fuel make the power it generates more expensive than power from an electric utility. A fuel powered generator is usually reserved to homes located a long distance from an electric utility, or where power interruptions are frequent, or where power interruptions would endanger the life of an occupant (such as a person relying on electrically powered life support medical equipment).

In recent years, windmill generators have begun to appear in the United States – though they reportedly have been common in Europe for years. They depend upon wind to generate electrical power, thereby requiring no fuel, creating no noise or exhaust fumes, and requiring almost no maintenance, making them an economical power generator and very environmentally friendly. Electrical power from windmill generators can be used in the house, and in some cases, *utility companies will buy the power from windmill generators*. However, they are quite visible since they need to be located higher than surrounding objects to be in the wind. Consequently, a home owner may find building restrictions on installing a windmill generator. Also, since a windmill generator depends upon wind of at least eight miles per hour to generate power, it will produce little or no power on days with little wind.

The windmill generator may be an ideal source of *supplemental electrical power* for your house. That is, it can silently generate electrical power day and night – provided there is some wind. But they should not be relied upon as the sole source of electrical power. Your house should also be connected to utility power. By doing so, the only electrical power you will need to pay for will be the power used in the house which is more than the windmill generator generates. And as mentioned previously, power generated by the windmill generator which exceeds the power used in the house may be purchased by the utility company.

With the ever increasing costs for energy, it is recommended that a windmill generator be given serious consideration. In doing so, four steps need to be taken:

1. Determine building code requirements in your locality to determine if a windmill generator is permissible and, if permissible, the requirements.

2. Determine the average wind speed in your locality. Your local weather bureau can provide this information. If the average wind speed is below about eight miles per hour, a windmill generator may not work well in your locality. Your

local distributor of windmill generators can provide guidance, as well as customer references, to you.

3.   Contact your electrical utility company to determine if they will purchase surplus electrical power from the generator; what they will pay; and electrical connection requirements. Your local windmill generator distributor can also provide assistance in this area.

4.   Consult with your architect and house inspector.

If you receive favorable responses for each step, a windmill generator may be a wise investment.

Fireplace

Fireplaces are a common feature in many houses today. It can be quite enjoyable to sit in front of a glowing fire on a cold winter evening, enjoying the warm radiant heat.

Though a fireplace can produce a lot of radiant heating, a lot of warm air from the house is also going up the chimney, day and night, whether there is a fire in the fireplace or not.[9] *On balance, there is more heat that goes out the chimney than the fireplace generates.* A fireplace *is not* an economical source of heat. Realizing this, though, if the enjoyment a fireplace will bring you outweighs the increased heating bills that heat loss out the chimney will bring, then by all means, go for it.

A relatively new "chimney-less" fireplace and gas logs have appeared. As the name implies, these are fireplaces fueled by gas (not wood) that have no chimney. This eliminates the heat loss created by warm air escaping through

---

[9] *Though almost all chimneys have a damper that is supposed to seal off the chimney when the fireplace is not in use, all of them that have been observed allowed air leakage when closed.*

the chimney. But it means the products of combustion from the fireplace are released into the house.

A typical gas fireplace is adjusted to produce a yellow flame like a wood fireplace (and not a blue flame typical for efficient, complete combustion of gas, as for a range burner). The products of combustion include carbon dioxide, water vapor, soot (the yellow flame is created by glowing carbon particles that are not fully burned), and probably carbon monoxide. Since there is no chimney to remove these products of combustion, they are released into the house. ***Therefore, a chimney-less fireplace is not recommended.***

Garage

The garage, of course, is intended to provide storage for automobiles, yard tools, children's toys, etc. By its nature, the floor quickly becomes covered with dirt, which is quickly tracked into the house if not promptly cleaned. The typical cure for this is to turn a hose on it.

Some house builders today are taking shortcuts that make this hazardous. Specifically, some houses are being built without a drain in the garage floor and without molding between the garage walls and the floor (see Figure 3 on page 68).

If you wash the garage floor in winter months and there is no drain, where will the water go? Well, it has to run out on the driveway. If the temperature is below freezing, the driveway will become a sheet of ice. In addition to being impossible to safely walk on, you will find it impossible to stop your car when backing out of the garage once it hits the driveway. Perhaps some builders stopped installing drains because of problems with them freezing in the winter in some localities. The cures for this are simple: (1) Install the drain closer to the house than the garage door so it will remain above freezing; (2) install the drain trap deeper in the floor below the freezing line.

Some house builders are also omitting the molding between the garage walls and the floor, obviously to cut costs. As a result, water from washing the floor may splash or seep through the wall and damage carpeting inside the house. Omission of the molding also leaves a path open for insects and mice to go from the garage into the house.

Be sure the molding is installed <u>and sealed at the bottom with a sealant</u> to prevent these problems.

<u>Also, be sure there is a good slope on the garage floor such that the house and walls are much higher than the drain (say, 0.7 inches)</u>. This will assure water will run to the drain and not collect in puddles.

Handicap Provisions

Surprisingly few houses are built with consideration for handicapped people. Perhaps this is due to most house buyers not being handicapped at the time they purchase their houses. However, many people, at some time in their lives, experience broken bones or other medical problems that require them to use a wheel chair or to be on crutches for a period of time. This is especially true for families with children who are active in sports. Have you ever tried to wheel a 29" wide wheel chair into a bathroom with a 28" wide doorway? Have you ever seen a person with a leg or hip injury try to move themselves from a wheel chair or crutches onto a toilet when there are no support bars in the bathroom to help them? By providing a few basic necessities, a house will become much more enjoyable for the handicapped person (whether temporarily or permanently handicapped) and also for the remainder of the family. The cost will be minimal. Following are suggested considerations.

1. Have at least one entrance to the house which has no steps, and which is wheel chair accessible. This will allow a person in a wheel chair to freely enter and exit the house without assistance.

2. Design the main floor of the house to have no steps.

3. Provide at least one bedroom on the main floor which is wheel chair accessible.

4. Provide a full bath on the main floor that is wheel chair accessible; has support bars on the walls to assist in the use of the toilet and shower; and has a walk-in shower.

Heating And Air Conditioning

There are two basic fuels commonly used today for heating houses, namely gas and electricity. Compressed natural gas and propane gas are sometimes used for houses located outside the service area of a natural gas utility. They require a storage tank at the house, and the fuel is periodically delivered by a fuel truck. Natural gas from a utility is more economical and reliable than the other gasses, and is the preferred gas.

Electricity is a "high grade" form of energy – that is, it can be used for many different purposes in many ways. The cost per energy unit for electricity from a utility is usually much higher than for natural gas (though, of course, if you generate your own electricity from the wind with a windmill generator, the cost of electricity will be very, very low, and will be less than for gas).

Electrical heating of a house can be accomplished by two methods, namely (1) direct resistance heaters (such as electric baseboard heaters) and (2) a heat pump. Direct resistance heating is a very inefficient use of electrical energy. Heating a house by this means may result in utility electric costs being three to four times as costly as natural gas. The cost to install baseboard electric heating, though, is much more economical than to install any other type of heating system.

The typical heat pump literally pumps heat from the air outside into the air inside your house. When the outside temperature drops below about 35 degrees, the air does not contain enough heat to enable the heat pump to produce adequate heat. When this occurs, a "heat strip" is automatically turned on, producing the additional heat needed. Since a heat strip is a resistance heater, it is not as efficient as the heat pump in generating heat. Consequently, a heat pump will heat a house for slightly less cost than an 80% efficient gas furnace as long as the outside air temperature is 35 degrees or more, depending upon the relative costs of gas and electricity. As the outside air temperature gets colder, the heat pump uses the heat strip more, and becomes less efficient. At some low temperature below 35 degrees, the heat pump will become more costly to operate than a gas furnace – particularly a gas furnace with 90% or more efficiency. Your local heating contractor can provide you with information on the projected annual heating costs for a gas furnace and for a heat pump. Installation cost of a heat pump is comparable to a gas furnace with 80% efficiency, and less costly than a gas furnace with 90% efficiency.

A geothermal heat pump might warrant consideration for your house. It is designed to pull heat from deep in the ground instead of from the air. Hence, it will operate efficiently regardless of outside air temperature and does not need to use an inefficient heat strip. But cost may be $4,000 to $9,000 more than a regular heat pump, depending on the size of your house and your location. Your local heating contractor can provide installation cost and heating cost estimates for a geothermal heat pump.

A heat pump with a blower will produce warm air that may be on the order of 100 degrees at the registers –

substantially below the 110 degrees or more typical at the registers with a gas furnace. As a result, a house heated with a heat pump and a warm air blower will feel cooler than a house with a gas furnace with a warm air blower, even if both houses are at the same temperature. Most people become accustomed to the cooler register air with the heat pump, though.

An alternative to heating by blown warm air is to heat by radiation (*this is not radioactive radiation*). Radiant heating is accomplished by having the heat from a heat pump or furnace heat water, and then have the hot water flow through small tubes in the floor, ceiling or walls of each room. Heat is radiated from this warm surface directly to a person's skin and clothing, and to furnishings in the room, thereby making them feel warm. Radiant heating does not use a blower, thereby eliminating any drafts, dust and noise.

Radiant floor heating will make the floor feel comfortably warm. But installation of carpeting in a room will make radiant floor heating less effective, and may make radiant floor heating virtually impossible. Hence, rooms that are fully covered with heavy carpet should use ceiling or wall radiant heating instead of floor radiant heating.

Radiant heating can be accomplished with either a gas furnace or a heat pump. It will be more expensive to purchase than a blower, duct and register system. But it will be quiet, draft – free, and cleaner. Your architect, house inspector or local heating contractor can provide you detailed information.

If your house will be located where home grown renewable natural fuel is abundant (such as corn, wood pellets or wood), you may want to consider installing a furnace or boiler that would burn these fuels. Naturally, the fuel is free, or nearly free. There are some model furnaces available that will operate for forty-eight hours on one load of wood. They can be attached to your blower system or hot water system and operate from your thermostat like any other furnace. They can also be coupled with a gas furnace or heat pump so that the gas furnace or heat pump will start automatically if the natural fuel furnace should run out of fuel. Your architect, house inspector, local heating contractor or general contractor can provide you with guidance on this.

The operating cost comparisons between a gas furnace and a regular heat pump (which pulls heat out of outside air) were made assuming that all electricity would be purchased from a utility company. If you install a windmill generator at your house, a significant part of the electricity used in your house may be generated by your generator, depending upon the size of the generator and its average output. For a house with a major portion of the electricity generated by a windmill generator, the cost for electricity to operate a heat pump would be very small, making it a much more economical method of heating than gas. A geothermal heat pump will produce the lowest operating cost, even if you purchase all of your electrical power. Again, your architect, house inspector, local heating contractor or general contractor can provide guidance.

Your architect can determine air conditioning requirements for your house. Before you decide on the amount of air conditioning needed, though, you may want to consider nature's natural air conditioners. Thick trellis vines near the house can lower the temperature at the outer walls of your house by ten degrees or more. Large trees located near the house[10] can also provide cooling as well as shade on the windows and roof. You may also want to consider installing attic vent fans and stapling low-emissivity, reflective foil under the roof rafters to reduce radiant heat transfer from a hot summer roof to the ceiling of your house. All of these will reduce the amount of air conditioning required, enabling you to save money by purchasing a smaller, less costly air

---

[10] *Large trees (including small trees that will become large in time) should be planted at least thirty feet from the house to minimize the possibility of damage from breaking limbs, etc.*

conditioning system and having smaller electric bills in the future.

Major utility cost savings can also be realized by installing an automatic thermostat system. In the winter, this system can be programmed to automatically increase the temperature before you get up in the morning; go to a lower temperature after you leave the house for work; increase the temperature just before you arrive home in the afternoon; and set to a lower temperature when you go to bed. In the summer, it would maintain the temperature at your desired level through the night; allow the house to become warmer (and less air conditioner running) while you are gone through the day; and reset to your desired temperature just before you arrive home in the afternoon. A programmable thermostat (which typically costs less than $200) can reduce utility costs and add comfort to your house, and should be given serious consideration.

Homeowner Associations And Covenants

Many housing additions have homeowner associations and covenants. The covenants limit and restrict the design of houses to certain standards; require the design for houses, fences, walls, pools, etc. be submitted to and approved by the homeowner's association before work is started; and provide for dues assessments.

Homeowner associations and covenants can be effective in maintaining the quality level of houses in an addition, and prevent erosion of the general quality of life in an addition by preventing undesirable conditions, such as someone operating a car repair shop out of their house or starting a dog kennel on their property, *but only under the right conditions.* Specifically, the properties must be owned by *individual homeowners* on a majority of the lots. The homeowner's association must also be active and enforce the covenants. If a majority of the properties are owned by one or two people (such as developers), the covenants may ultimately provide no protection to the homeowners. Being a majority of the property owners in an addition, the developers may be able to change the covenants at will to suit themselves, and possibly to the detriment of the homeowners.

As an example, the author built a house in Wildwood Estates south of Fayetteville, Georgia. When he started construction, 47 of the 74 lots in the addition were owned by the developer. One of the covenants required that all houses have an all brick exterior. His house was built accordingly.

A few years later, a house was built next door with siding instead of brick. When the author complained, he was told the covenants of the homeowner's association had been changed to permit siding instead of brick "by a majority of the property owners". Who was the "majority"? It was the developer, who owned 47 of the 74 lots. To the author's knowledge, the 27 homeowners who lived in this addition had no voice in this change.

Kitchen Design

This section presents kitchen design features for your consideration. The items are presented in alphabetical order.

Counter Space

Counter space is often inadequate in a kitchen. This becomes painfully obvious when a multi-course meal is being prepared for several people. The useable counter length should be at least sixteen feet. The length of the sink and range, of course, is not considered useable counter length.

Range

Most people have a preference for the type of range. Some prefer gas. Others prefer electric. Our purpose here is to make you aware of some of the developments that have taken place recently on both types of ranges.

Gas range manufacturers have developed pilot-less electrical ignition systems for burners and ovens. My experience has shown they usually work fine. Occasionally, though, the sparking igniter (which operates like a spark plug in an automobile) will not ignite a burner. This is often due to debris blocking the path for gas flow to the igniter, or something spilled on the sparking igniter, shorting it out and causing it to not spark. Remove any debris from the gas passages. Carefully scrub the igniter clean with a *non-metal* scrubber (use of a metal scouring pad may damage the igniter or short it out by leaving metal residue on the igniter). This usually corrects the problem.

Gas range manufacturers have developed iron pan supports over the burners which are coated with a non-stick surface (see Figure 6). My experience has shown the non-stick coating on the supports is very durable and effective. However, spills on the support must be scrubbed off with a scouring pad. Throwing them into a dish washer will not thoroughly clean them. With the many intricate curves and surfaces, scouring a support is a time-consuming, laborious chore.

Unfortunately, the non-stick coating presents a safety hazard. Certain smooth bottom pans slide very easily on the burner support, making it very easy for these pans to slide off the stove and on to the floor. ***This is a potential safety hazard. A stove with this type of support is not recommended.***

Since gas can produce heat directly at a lower cost than electricity, it would seem that a gas range would operate more economically than an electric range. However, a gas range allows a large amount of the heat from a burner to escape around the side of a pan instead of heating a pan. This greatly decreases the efficiency of a gas range. Hence, the cost of operating an electric range may be very comparable to that of a gas range.

Electric range manufacturers have developed new smooth top cooking surfaces and new type heating systems, making them very easy to clean, and much faster heating than the old calrod type burners. The different types of stoves and their features are too numerous to present here. It is recommended that you visit appliance stores to learn of the features and benefits of electric and gas ranges before you make your purchase. Your architect, house inspector, and *Consumer Reports* magazine may also be able to provide you guidance.

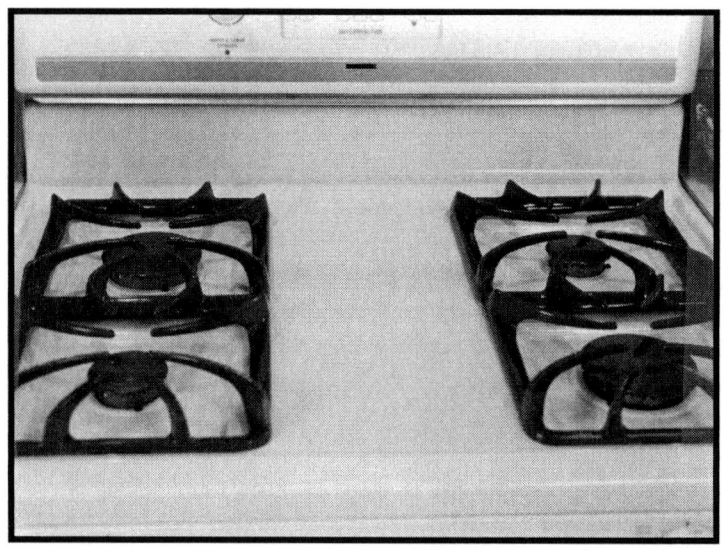

Figure 6
Top Of Gas Range With Non – Stick Pan Supports

Vent Fan

The purpose of a vent fan is to remove the heat and steam generated by cooking. Unfortunately, some "vent fans" installed in kitchens today do not vent at all. They only make noise, and take the heat and steam from cooking on the range and blow it toward the ceiling and back into the kitchen, thereby doing no good. Your architect should make sure that a true kitchen vent fan (one that exhausts hot, steamy air outside the house) is specified. Your house inspector should inspect and confirm the proper vent fan system has been installed and properly vented to the exterior of the house.

Lighting – Indirect Fluorescent

Indirect fluorescent lighting has many benefits: soft, shadow free lighting; no glare; better color than standard incandescent light bulbs; approximately ten times the life of a standard incandescent light bulb; and requires about ¼ the electricity required by a standard incandescent light bulb for the same amount of lighting. They are more costly to install, though. Overall, they offer more enjoyable lighting with less maintenance, and merit consideration. Indirect fluorescent lighting is recommended and should be discussed with your architect and house inspector.

Paint

The kitchen and bathrooms are especially hard on paints. If standard flat wall paints are used, the walls will be easily stained, very difficult or impossible to wash clean, and the paint will deteriorate in a short time.

It is recommended that these rooms be painted with semi-gloss latex enamel paints which are specifically designed for high humidity environments. These paints are very washable and hold up much better than a standard flat paint, thereby retaining an excellent appearance and not requiring repainting as often as with other paints.

If you are designing a new house or purchasing a newly built house, the builder will probably try to talk you out of applying a semi-gloss paint in these rooms, saying it would not look good. The builder may be correct – but it would be due to the builder not properly finishing the walls prior to painting and not properly painting the walls. Many builders do not fill and sand walls thoroughly, leaving small indentations and imperfections where there are nails or drywall tape. They will then cover a poorly finished wall with one thick coat of a flat latex paint. The wall imperfections will not be very noticeable. However, applying a semi-gloss paint would make the imperfections very noticeable.

The walls should be properly filled and sanded prior to painting. A coat of primer/sealer paint should then be applied. This should be followed with one or two coats of semi-gloss latex enamel paint. Obviously, this requires much more labor and materials than most builders put into finishing a kitchen or bathrooms. The vastly superior appearance, washability and durability, though, make it worthwhile.

Pool And Jacuzzi

A swimming pool and a jacuzzi can provide a lot of enjoyment for you and your family. If not designed and installed properly, though, they can be dangerous and expensive.

Be sure to use an experienced, licensed, reputable contractor to install and service your pool and jacuzzi. Your architect, attorney, house inspector and Better Business Bureau can provide guidance.

It is recommended that a solar heating system be used to heat your pool. Although gas heaters are sometimes used, they will increase your gas bills significantly. Solar heating is free (almost), after the cost of installing the solar heating system.

Great care must be exercised when installing the drain or pump return outlets in a pool or jacuzzi. If a single return is installed while the pump is operating or drain is open, it is possible for an occupant to be held down against the return outlet on the bottom. Hence, at least two large return or drain inlets should be installed a distance apart such that one person cannot block both outlets.

Outlet covers should be sufficiently large to prevent a person from being held down against an outlet if the pump is operating or the drain is open. Your house inspector, pool contractor, and building codes can provide the guidance needed.

Private Mortgage Insurance

Private mortgage insurance is obviously not part of a house design, but is part of a house's financial package that many people are paying for needlessly today. Private mortgage insurance (called "PMI") protects the *mortgage company* in case a homeowner defaults on their mortgage. It provides *no benefit* to the homeowner. Mortgage companies typically require homeowners to purchase PMI if they have less than 20% equity in their house. Hence, a person making a 15% down payment on their house would be required to purchase this insurance. After making house payments for a period of time, a homeowner's equity will reach 20% of the purchase price, and PMI insurance is no longer required. However, there are many cases where PMI insurance is continued needlessly and the homeowner is charged $300 to $1,000 annually for the insurance premiums. Therefore, it is recommended that you mark the payment and date on your amortization schedule (which should be provided by your mortgage company) when you will achieve 20% equity on the purchase price of your house. On that date, ask your mortgage company to cancel the PMI insurance. If they refuse, consult with your attorney.

Roof Material

Most houses are built with asphalt shingles. Some are built with wood shingles. And some are built with a metal roof. Asphalt and wood shingle roofs are most economical to install, but they deteriorate and need to be repaired periodically and replaced in ten to thirty years, depending upon the initial quality of the shingles and the weather conditions in your location. A metal roof, on the other hand, can be expected to last for fifty years to a lifetime.

A metal roof is not flammable, like asphalt or wood shingles. Hence, a house with a metal roof is likely to have lower insurance premiums. Finally, a metal roof will reflect the heat from the sun much better than wood or asphalt shingles, thereby reducing your utility cost for air conditioning.

In summary, a metal roof costs more to install, but it will be a lower cost roof in the long run. Incidentally, a metal roof can be installed over an existing shingle roof without having to remove the shingles.

There is an aluminum roof available with a special heat barrier paint for maximum rejection of the sun's summer heat, providing you maximum savings on air conditioning utility expenses. For more details, consult your architect, house inspector, general contractor or a roofing contractor.

Shape of your house

The shape of your house will have a significant effect on your heating and air conditioning expenses, as well as the cost of the house. A house designed to minimize the outside wall area will require the least amount of heating and air conditioning, thereby minimizing utility expenses. It will also require the least amount of materials to construct, resulting in a lower purchase price. A single story house that is perfectly round will have the minimum outside wall area. A perfectly square house of the same square feet will have 13% more outside wall area. A single floor ranch style house may have 28% more outside wall area than a round house, depending on the exact length versus width. A two story house will have even more outside wall area. Therefore, selecting a house that is one story and perfectly round will afford you minimum utility expenses for heating and air conditioning.

Although a round house will require the least amount of materials, the added complexity to construct may offset any savings in materials. If a round house is not for you, you may want to consider a single story house which is close to square in shape. The houses to avoid are a very long house which is very narrow, and a two story house. They will be the most costly to buy, to heat, and to air condition.

Veterans Administration Guaranteed Loans

Though this is not a part of the house design, it is a very important part of the financial package that you may be considering. Basically, a Veterans' Administration Guaranteed Loan will enable you to purchase a house without a down payment. But you will not get this for free. A V.A. loan will cost 2% of the total loan if this is your first V.A. loan, or 3% if this is your second V.A. loan.

Suppose you were planning to purchase a house for $180,000 and you were going to obtain a V.A. guaranteed loan for the first time to finance it. After filling out many documents and incurring higher fees from your attorney for his/her additional work, your loan may be approved. From Table 1 on page 3, the total expenses at closing would be $10,784 plus the V.A. fee of 2% of the loan. Thus, your mortgage would be $194,678 as shown below:

House purchase price	$180,000
Closing costs per Table 1	$ 10,784
V.A. loan fee	$ 3,894
Total Mortgage:	$194,678

With an interest rate of 8% on the mortgage, monthly payments would be $1,428.55 for principal and interest. This is substantially more than the $1,188.76 monthly payment with 10% down payment, as shown in Table 5 on page 19.

At closing with a V.A. loan, you would need to pay virtually nothing, assuming the closing costs and V.A. loan fee were wrapped into your mortgage. The person without the V.A. loan who makes a 10% down payment on his house would have paid $28,784 at loan closing.

With the V.A. loan as above, you will pay $86,324.40 more in house payments over the thirty year life of the mortgage than the person who did not have a V.A. loan and made a 10% down payment.

To put this into one concise sentence: If you purchase a $180,000 house with a V.A. guaranteed loan with no down payment instead of a conventional loan with a 10% down payment, you will pay $28,784 less at closing of the mortgage, but will have substantially higher monthly payments and pay $86,324.40 more in house payments over the thirty year life of the mortgage.

It is, therefore, recommended that conventional financing with a down payment be used instead of a V.A. guaranteed loan with no down payment. Perhaps this will require a delay in purchasing a house in order to save for a down payment. But it will save you money in the long run.

Water Heaters

It has been common practice to install one water heater of approximately 40 gallons capacity to provide hot water for an entire house. Today, a new type of water heater is available. It is called a "point-of-use" or "tank-less" water heater. As the name implies, a "point-of-use" water heater is installed precisely where the hot water will be used. There typically will be a "point-of-use" water heater for each bathroom, one for the kitchen and dish washer, etc. They are very small compared to the old type tank water heater with some models capable of being installed under a sink.

Though "point-of-use" water heaters may cost more to purchase than the old tank type water heater, the "point-of-use" water heaters are much more efficient, resulting in substantially lower utility bills. "Point-of-use" water heaters also provide hot water instantly at a tap. You will not have to run three gallons of water through the tap to get hot water, as is often the case with the tank type water heater.

It is suggested that you discuss "point-of-use" water heaters with your architect, house inspector and plumbing contractor for further guidance.

Water Pipe Insulation

All water pipes should be covered with an insulation jacket. This is especially important for a house with one large water heater, as this will prevent the hot water from being cooled quickly between the water heater and each water tap. It will also prevent moisture from condensing on cold water pipes and dripping onto the basement floor.

Windows

Windows provide a means of enjoying the scenery outside the house. They also brighten a room by letting sunlight in. They do a lot to make a house enjoyable.

Windows can also do a lot to make a house *un*-enjoyable. In winter months, they can leak cold air into the house and condense moisture on them and the casing (especially aluminum casings). In summer, they can leak warm air, pollens and dust into the house; allow house heating via solar radiation; and cause materials to fade due to admittance of ultraviolet light. More heat can be lost through two 36" x 72" windows than through an entire outside wall of a room in the winter. In summer, *one* 36" x 72" window can provide more heating in a room than an entire outside wall of a room. Hence, in addition to discomfort, windows increase utility costs dramatically.

Through careful selection of windows and placement of trees,[11] these problems can be minimized. Wood and aluminum materials should be avoided for window frames. Wood frames require maintenance. Aluminum frames will conduct heat into the house in summer and out in winter, and will cause moisture to condense on them in the winter. Vinyl or fiberglass window frames should be used. These materials are good insulators of heat; will resist condensing moisture in the winter; reduce air leakage; and are maintenance free. Additionally, double pane, high performance "sun insulating" windows are recommended to further reduce heat transfer

---

[11] *Trees located to provide shade on windows during the peak heating period of the day will greatly reduce solar heating and material fading in the house. In winter, when leaves fall from the trees, the windows will be exposed to sunlight, allowing solar warming. Large trees (including small trees that will become large trees in time) should be located at least thirty from the house to minimize the possibility of damage due to breaking limbs, etc.*

through the window and to filter out ultraviolet light, thereby reducing sun fading of materials in the house.

Selection of good windows will cost more than lower quality windows. The reward, though, is much more enjoyment of your house; a more quiet, draft-free, dust- and pollen-free house; lower utility expenses; and less interior damage due to materials fading from the sun.

Yard Watering Systems

Most people water their yards by the traditional hose and sprinkler. This is the best way for lawns that are smaller than 10,000 square feet.

If your yard is 10,000 square feet or larger, you may want to consider a separate water meter for your outside water faucets. When you use water from your normal water meter, there is a sewage fee charged for the water you use. Usually the sewage fee costs more than the water. But when you water your lawn, none of this water returns to the sewage treatment plant. Hence, many cities will allow the outside faucets to be connected to a separate meter and not charge for sewage on that meter.

The cost to install a second meter will be about $600, and the monthly charge for the meter will be about $6.00 (costs, of course, will vary with locality and water quantity used). With a 10,000 square foot yard that requires watering about four times per month for five months each year, a separate meter will begin to save you money after about 2 ½ years (and sooner with a larger yard).

You may also want to consider an irrigation system (where sprinkler heads are buried in the grass). Cost varies widely, depending on the size and shape of your yard. Cost would be around $4,500 for a 10,000 square foot yard.

Your architect, house inspector, and general contractor can provide more detailed information.

CHAPTER 7

SAFETY AND SECURITY

Safety and security in the house are often given very little consideration until something happens. This chapter presents special features that have a major impact on safety and security, and merit consideration whether you are purchasing an existing house or designing a new house. Many are also applicable to your present house or apartment. The features are presented in alphabetical order.

Bathroom Floor

Bathroom floors are usually either a vinyl tile, a masonry type tile, or carpet. Each has a serious safety defect.

The vinyl and masonry type tiles typically become very slippery when wet, making it very easy for a person coming from the bathtub or shower to slip and fall.

Carpeting eliminates the problem of being slippery when wet, and will not feel cold to bare feet like tiles. But it is virtually impossible to clean the carpeting thoroughly, making it a source of diseases and odors.

The best floor material would be a masonry or vinyl tile which has an anti-slip surface. An effective anti-slip surface will feel almost like sandpaper to the hand. A surface that has raised areas but which will allow your hand to slide over it easily when wet is likely to _not_ be an effective anti-slip surface. Your architect, house inspector and general contractor can give you further advice on available materials.

Carbon Monoxide Detectors

Carbon monoxide is a colorless, odorless gas that is created when a fuel (such as gas, wood, oil, etc.) is burned. It can enter a house by a defect in a gas furnace, gas water heater, gas clothes dryer, or a fireplace. An automobile left running in an attached garage can also cause carbon monoxide to build up in a house. When a person is exposed to a sufficient concentration of carbon monoxide for a period of time, it will cause death.

Carbon monoxide detectors installed in your house will provide a warning of the presence of carbon monoxide before the level becomes dangerous, enabling you and your family to safely leave the house.

Carbon monoxide detectors can be purchased individually for less than $50. Some security systems may also include them with their system. Consult with your house inspector for his advice.

Fire Extinguishers

At least one fire extinguisher is usually required in a house by insurance companies in order to get the best insurance rate. In the author's opinion, one is not enough. There should be a fire extinguisher mounted near each entrance to the kitchen. There should be a fire extinguisher mounted near the entrance to the garage. There should also be a fire extinguisher mounted near the entrance to each bedroom. Each fire extinguisher should have a rating of 3-A:10-B:C. It will be a dry chemical extinguisher suitable for trash, wood, paper, liquid grease, or electrical fires, and will weigh about nine pounds fully charged.

This is not intended to make you a professional fire fighter. It is intended to make an extinguisher immediately available to you in case of a _small fire that can be quickly extinguished._ If you had just one extinguisher in the house and it was located near the range with a grease fire in the kitchen, it might be impossible for you to reach that extinguisher. Likewise, if someone fell asleep while smoking in bed and set bedding on fire, you need a fire extinguisher located right there to enable you to act immediately. Having to run to the kitchen for an extinguisher and then return to the burning bedroom would be a poor, dangerous act that could cost the life of the person in bed as well as the person trying to help.

Perhaps the best fire prevention system would be a central sprinkler system. Without question, it would be expensive. But it would be very effective in preventing a serious fire and injuries or loss of life to you and your family. A premium discount on your homeowner's insurance may also be offered by your insurance company. Your architect, house inspector or general contractor can provide more information.

<u>Garage</u>

Garage windows enable people to see into your garage and determine if your cars are gone. If there is no car in the garage, thieves will interpret this to mean no one is home and your house is an easy target. This can be prevented by having no windows in the garage. If this is not a satisfactory solution, you may want to consider installing the windows high on the garage walls such that no one can look in and observe whether your cars are there or not. Another alternative is to put heavy curtains over the windows (curtains that you cannot see through).

Garage doors equipped with electric garage door openers are equipped with an emergency release cord near the door, as shown in Figure 7. If there should be a power outage or a failure of the garage door opener, the door cannot be opened by normal means. By pulling on the emergency release cord, though, the door is disconnected from the garage door opener, and can be opened by simply pulling up on the door. Thieves know this too. Hence, a common means of breaking into a garage is to break a garage door window, pull on the emergency release cord, and pull the door up. Note how close the emergency release is to the garage door window in Figure 7.

The best method to prevent thieves from entering your garage in this manner is to not have any windows in your garage door. An alternative, and perhaps less effective, method is to shorten the emergency release cord as much as possible, as shown in Figure 8, placing the cord out of their reach through the window. Naturally, if they stand on something outside the door, they still may be able to reach the emergency release cord.

Incidentally, placing tools (such as drills, electric saws, etc.) on display shows everyone what you have available for stealing. It is an invitation for theft. Your tools will be much more secure if kept out of sight, preferably in locked cabinets.

House builders often like to make the concrete very smooth on garage floors. This may make it look nice, and may be a little easier to clean. But it also makes the floor extremely slippery when wet, making it very easy to fall and sustain injuries. It is strongly recommended the garage floor be finished with some roughness. Naturally, the driveway and sidewalks should be (and usually are) finished with some roughness for the same reason.

Figure 7

Figure 8

Keyless Entry Door Locks

Keyless entry door locks is a convenient system and eliminates the problems of searching for the right key and getting it properly installed in the door in the dark. And no more problems with lost or misplaced keys. For further information, contact your architect, house inspector or general contractor.

Incidentally, if you are purchasing a house that has been previously owned, the first thing you need to do upon taking possession of your house is to call a locksmith and have all the door locks changed. Perhaps the previous owner gave you all the keys *he* had to your house. But what about any children, relatives, previous owners before him, etc? Changing all locks is not a very expensive or time consuming chore, and it eliminates any unknown person from having a key to your house. And don't forget to change the code on your security system and the electric garage door opener. The previous owner should have papers that tell how to do this. If these papers are not available or you have questions, the company that monitors your security system and the installer of the electric garage door opener can assist you.

Lightning Protection

A complete lightning protection system consists of two sub-systems: a lightning rod system, which provides protection from a direct lightning strike on the house; and a surge suppression system for the house electrical system, which provides protection from the effects of a nearby lightning strike. Both are needed to provide good protection to a house, its occupants, the house electrical system and electrical equipment in the house. The surge suppression system is discussed in more detail on page 120.

When the term "lightning rod" is used, many people envision big, ugly spikes sitting on top of farm houses and barns. While lightning rods were tall and unsightly in the past, they have become much smaller today. Their applications now include buildings and houses in cities – and for good reason. Each year, according to the National Lightning Safety Institute, lightning causes more deaths and injuries than tornadoes and hurricanes combined. And it causes 30,190 house fires and $175,200,000 in damages to residences in the United States annually.

Figure 9 is a picture of a house within the city of Fort Wayne, Indiana. It was probably built after 1990. I admired this beautiful house when I took the picture. But I took the picture for a special reason. This house is equipped with ten lightning rods. But they cannot be seen in the picture, can they? In fact, they were almost invisible to me when standing in the front yard of the house.

Although the lightning protection system is not very complex, it must include only Underwriter's Laboratory listed equipment and be installed by an Underwriter's Laboratory approved company. This is not a "do-it-yourself" project. Failure to do this may result in the installation of an unsafe system and result in damage to your house and injury to you and your family. Your architect or house inspector may be able to provide guidance to an appropriate company.

Does installation of a lightning protection system with a full house surge protection system guarantee lightning will not strike your house, and guarantee your house will not be damaged from a nearby lightning strike? The answer is an emphatic ***NO!*** The lightning protection system *greatly reduces the chances* of a lightning strike or an electrical surge causing damage in a house, but it does not guarantee it cannot happen. Lightning has tremendous power, and man does not yet fully understand it. Sometimes it will do unexpected things, in spite of man's best efforts. Below are a few examples.

Figure 9

In the late 1770's, Benjamin Franklin (the inventor of the lightning rod) was asked to design a lightning rod to protect the dome of the State House in Annapolis, Maryland, as it had been damaged by lightning previously. After installation of the lightning rod, lightning did strike the State House – but only once in 208 years.

In Chicago, Illinois, a housewife was home alone when a thunderstorm occurred. While she was in the bathroom, lightning struck a tree in her yard. The electricity from the bolt followed the tree roots to water and sewer pipes, and followed them back into the woman's house, knocking her off the toilet and doing major damage to the house. In hindsight (no pun intended), a reader with an unbridled sense of humor might be inclined to chuckle. But it really is not humorous. If the woman had been washing her hands, or had been taking a bath or shower, she might well have been electrocuted. And since the house was not struck by lightning, and the power of the lightning did not come in on the power lines, telephone lines or cable television wires, a lightning protection system with lightning rods and a surge suppressor would not have prevented this from happening.

In the summer of 1996, Mrs. Isabel Nunemaker was at her desk in her lakefront home in Edwardsburg, Michigan. A typical summer storm was taking place outside – nothing severe. Suddenly, her desk light exploded with a blinding flash. She immediately smelled burning wires. No, her house had not been struck by lightning. Lightning had struck a tree in the neighbor's yard and then jumped over to her power lines that were several yards from the tree. Though there was no fire, all wiring in her house was burned up. All appliances that were plugged in were also destroyed. If a surge protection system had been installed, there may well have been little or no damage.

Installation of a lightning protection system is a very wise investment, regardless of where your house is located. The cost will be in the range of $2,000 or more, depending upon the size and shape of your house, and the equipment included in the lightning protection system. However, it is likely your insurance company will reduce your homeowner's insurance premiums with the installation of a complete lightning protection system (lightning rods and a surge protection system for the entire house) that is a U.L. approved system.

Radon Gas

Radon gas is a colorless, odorless radioactive gas that comes from the ground. It is the second largest cause of lung cancer, killing about 22,000 people each year.

Since radon gas comes from the ground, this hazard is determined mostly by where your house is located and not by the design of the house. However, it is logical that houses with a basement or a crawl space would be at most risk for radon gas.

Tests can be performed to determine if radon gas is present. If radon gas is shown to be present, a corrective ventilation system can be installed for less than $1,800.

Security Lights

Security lights can help to deter a break-in at your home, and also provide lighting when you return home after dark. It is suggested the lights be installed high and be protected so that a person with criminal intent cannot reach up and remove the bulb or break it with a hammer or stone. It is also recommended that the lights be controlled by a light detector and a motion detector such that they will turn on automatically at night and only if motion is detected in the yard. This will extend the life of the light bulbs and minimize your utility expenses.

Security System

A security system will warn you if a door is opened, a window is opened, or there is anyone moving in the house, or when a fire is detected. The system will also automatically call your security monitoring company and report the detected problem.[12]

Security systems are such an effective crime deterrent and fire detection system that insurance companies provide

---

[12] *Be sure that the security system you purchase is programmed to automatically call your security monitoring company in case of a fire, break-in, etc. It should not call the police or fire department. Security systems will occasionally send a false alarm that there is trouble when there is no trouble. Consequently, some cities – including Baltimore, Las Vegas and Salt Lake City – will not respond to security system alarms unless they are verified by a private security guard, a surveillance camera or the resident. Other cities – including Chicago, Los Angeles and New York – give alarm calls a low priority, meaning that it may be an hour or more before they respond. Consequently, the security system must be programmed to notify a security monitoring company who will respond promptly to an emergency message from your security system; verify that the message is valid; and then notify authorities.*

discounts to homeowners with houses equipped with them. Their cost varies widely, depending on the size of your house and how elaborate the system is that you want, but is typically in the $200 to $400 range. Your architect, house inspector or general contractor can provide more detailed information on the systems available and recommend a dependable, reputable security system company to you.

One word of caution. Some security companies will install sensors on ground floor windows to sense when they are opened, but provide nothing for second floor windows on a two story house.

Apparently they assume that no one would consider putting a ladder up against the house to reach second floor windows. In the writer's opinion, this is a foolish risk. All windows should be equipped with security sensors.

Surge Suppression

A voltage surge is the temporary presence of excessive voltage in the wiring in the house. It can be caused by a storm many miles away, or the operation of electrical appliances in your house. It may be only a few volts, or it can sometimes be several thousand volts. It normally lasts for only a few thousandths of a second. A person operating a motor powered appliance, such as a sweeper, will not notice any effect from a surge. Likewise, a surge usually occurs so rapidly that you will not see any flicker of light bulbs. However, surges can shorten the life of light bulbs, and certain electrical equipment which is very sensitive to voltage surges can be damaged or destroyed.

A typical house today has many, many electrical devices that contain very delicate electronic control systems. Examples include television sets, video cassette recorders, stereo, radios, clocks, telephones, refrigerators, ranges, microwave ovens, furnace/air conditioning systems, garage door openers, computers, smoke and fire alarms, etc. The electronic controls in many of these systems can be damaged by a voltage surge of only one or two volts. The manufacturers of these devices recognize there will be voltage surges in a house and protect their circuits from *minor* surges. But they are almost never protected from a major surge. When a major surge occurs, the homeowner may not realize it at the time it occurs. All he will know is that, suddenly for some unknown reason, the computer quit working; or the television quit working; or the microwave quit working; etc. Strange as it may seem, a major voltage surge may knock out certain electrical equipment immediately; may damage other equipment, but they may continue to operate normally for a short period of time; and may not damage other equipment at all.

Surge suppressors have been developed which can provide protection to an entire house. When a surge appears on power lines, the suppressor is designed to absorb it, protecting all electrical equipment in your house.

Some surge protection manufacturers also provide insurance protection against surge damage to your electrical equipment. If there is an extremely strong surge, the suppressor may burn out, but should protect everything in your house from the surge. Naturally, a surge suppressor will not provide protection against a direct lightning strike. Properly installed lightning rods will minimize the risk of a direct strike. See Lightning Protection on page 115.

A surge suppressor that will protect the entire house is strongly recommended. The surge suppressor should be designed to also provide surge protection for all telephone lines and cable television lines. Extremely sensitive circuits (such as your computer, television and VCR) should each be provided a small surge protector which will provide surge protection on all power wires, telephone wires, cable TV wires, etc. that are connected to these devices.

Your architect, house inspector, reputable electrical contractor, or your electric utility company can provide you with additional guidance. Also, see Lightning Protection on page 115, as surge suppressors are often part of a lightning protection system.

Swimming Pool Or Jacuzzi

All swimming pools and jacuzzis have a drain or pump return outlet at the bottom. When water is draining or the pump is operating, an incredible downward force can be exerted on a person if they cover this outlet and this is the only outlet for the pump or drain. There have been cases where people have been held on the bottom under water, unable to move against this force.

The pump return or drain should have at least two outlets at the bottom that are connected together and separated by an appropriate distance such that a person cannot block both outlets. The outlets should be designed such that a person cannot be held to an outlet in case they cover one of them while the pump or drain is operating. Your architect and house inspector can provide you with the local building code requirements and the appropriate design.

Telephone Junction Box

Contractors typically install the telephone junction box on the outside of a house, as shown in Figure 10. This is nice and convenient for a telephone repairman. It also enables a criminal to cut the telephone wires, making your security system unable to notify your security company of a break-in or fire, and disabling your telephone.

The solution is to *hide* this junction box inside your garage. By doing this, a criminal cannot disable your security system or telephone, even if successful in breaking into your garage. Though this may make more work for the telephone company if repairs are needed, they will be understanding of your reason for this. Your telephone company can do this for you.

Figure 10

Windows Located Next To Entry Doors

Many houses are designed with some sort of window next to an entry door, as shown in Figure 11. Though this has a nice appearance, it enables a person to easily break into a house by breaking the small window next to the door, and then reach in and unlock the door.

It is much more safe to locate windows away from the door locks so that it is impossible for someone to break a window and reach in and unlock the door.

Some houses are equipped with dead bolts that require a key to unlock from the inside as well as the outside. There is an inherent danger in doing this. If there would be a fire and people would try to exit through the door, they would not be able to open the door without a key to the dead bolt. For this reason, dead bolts which require a key to unlock from the inside are illegal in many localities, and should be avoided.

Figure 11

CHAPTER 8

THE IMPOSSIBLE HAPPENS: FINANCIAL CRISIS

Suppose a family has followed the advice provided in this book to the letter. Suppose the wife's take-home pay is $1,300 per month and the husband's take-home pay is $4,500 per month, producing a total take-home pay of $5,800 per month. Their total financial analysis (chapter 2, page 25) showed they have total expenses (Item 5 on Table 6, page 31) of $5,500 per month, producing a cash reserve of $300 per month, and have faithfully saved this $300 per month for the four years they have owned their home and now totals $15,000 in the bank. It would be easy for them to feel carefree – that there is no chance of any financial problems. Unfortunately, that is not the case.

Suppose the husband loses his job. His take-home pay will drop to zero for two weeks, and then he will be able to receive unemployment compensation checks of, say $300 per week for a *maximum* of twenty-six weeks.[13] The husband's health insurance most likely will also stop (which will mean no health insurance for anyone in the family), unless there is a decision to continue it as provided by COBRA. Lets assume their decision is to continue this insurance, and the cost is $600 per month.

For the first two weeks of unemployment, the family take-home pay will be reduced to the wife's take-home pay of $300 per week, or a total of $600 for the two weeks. Expenses will continue at $5,500 per month (which is equal to $2,538 for the two weeks). And now there will be the additional cost for health insurance of $600 per month (which is equal to $278

---

[13] *Unemployment compensation provisions vary from state to state. The values cited here are considered typical.*

for the two weeks). For these first two weeks of unemployment, there will be $600 of income and $2,816 of expenses. Expenses will exceed income by $2,216 for these first two weeks. Where will the money come from to pay these bills? Well, it will have to come from the $15,000 cash reserve that has been saved. Hence, after just two weeks, $2,216 will need to be withdrawn from the $15,000 cash reserve that has been saved. The cash reserve will be reduced from $15,000 to $12,784.

During the third through the twelfth week of unemployment, take home income will be $300 per week for the wife and $300 per week unemployment compensation for the husband for a total of $600 per week, or a total of $6,000 for this ten week period. Expenses for this period will be $14,080. This will require withdrawing an additional ($14,080 - $6,000), or $8,080 from the cash reserve, reducing it to $4,704.

Obviously, the family cannot continue to operate with this deficiency in income. In fact, at this rate, they will run out of money in another four weeks. Then what?

This dilemma happens to many people every day. It happens to very wealthy people who have planned their financial lives carefully as well as to the average person. It is often caused by factors beyond their control. It is frustrating. It is embarrassing. It is also something that must be faced squarely by anyone who experiences this situation and corrective steps taken *immediately*. Failure to do so may cause a family to lose their home to foreclosure and possibly face bankruptcy.

First of all, a family must prepare in advance for this type of emergency by maintaining a cash reserve sufficient to enable them to meet all expenses for at least three months. This cash reserve may be a savings plan that will pay them interest. As soon as a family becomes aware their income is likely to decrease sharply, they should *immediately* make a current financial analysis, as shown on Table 7 (pages 37, 38 and 39). This will show how much expenses would be exceeding their income (that is, Item 5 will exceed Item 1 in this table – a condition that must be avoided). Then the following steps should be taken immediately:

1. Identify expenditures that can be eliminated temporarily – and do so. This may include cable television, clothing expenditures, personal entertainment (restaurants, theaters, golf, travel, magazine subscriptions), lawn service, cellular telephones, elective medical services (including routine dental work), house repairs, etc.

2. Reduce utility expenses by setting the air conditioning temperature to a warmer setting or setting the heat to a cooler temperature; eliminate watering of yards totally.

3. Reduce grocery expenses by purchasing less costly foods (e.g., hamburger instead of steaks; more meatless meals and low cost meals); no treat foods (ice cream, desserts, potato chips, etc.).

4. Eliminate the purchases of alcoholic beverages and carbonated beverages.

5. Temporarily stop saving toward anticipated future expenses (Item 4 in Table 7).

These steps *must be taken aggressively and immediately.* They will be uncomfortable to take. We are talking about survival without permanent damage, though. This needs to be done thoroughly, aggressively and immediately.

After taking these steps, construct a new total financial analysis per Table 7. If your cash reserve is a positive number, then you have balanced your budget. Your income will exceed your expenses. No further action is needed, except to be sure to keep expenditures within your new budget. You may find, though, that you still have expenses exceeding your income (that is, the cash reserve in Table 7 will be a negative number). This negative number is the minimum amount you must increase your income in order to break even for a short period of time (that is, for up to perhaps nine months).

Increasing income can be accomplished by increasing the hours of work by the working spouse, and by the unemployed spouse becoming employed. In bad economic periods, of course, these steps may be difficult to achieve and may require months to do. If this cannot be done within a few weeks, there is another step that must be taken *immediately.*

Call your creditors (mortgage company; bank with whom you have a bank loan; credit card companies; etc.) as soon as you see that you will continue to have a negative cash reserve for more than a few weeks. *Tell them the truth about your situation*. Request an extension on your mortgage payments, your car payments, credit card payments, etc. Ask your utility companies to put you on a deferred payment plan, if available. If you have maintained good credit and are current on your payments to your creditors, most of them will work with you *and will respect you for being honest.*

This will buy you time to find employment and increase your income.

It is very critical that you talk with your creditors before you get behind in payments. Once you are behind, they may not grant you an extension or be as willing to work with you.

You may also want to investigate the possibility of borrowing against the equity in your house or life insurance. If you are able to do this, the cash obtained will buy you time to find additional income.

It would be wise to consult with a credit counseling company to help you restructure your financial program. Your Better Business Bureau can recommend reputable companies in your area that will charge little or nothing for their service.

It is embarrassing and frustrating to go hat in hand to creditors and ask for their help. But it is really the best thing you can do. By doing this, it will show your creditors that you _recognize_ you have a problem; that you are _being honest with them_; and _you are working hard to get back on track._[14] They will respect you for your honesty, candidness and efforts, and will almost always make every effort to work with you.

In rare circumstances, you may find that, after being granted an extension by a creditor, you are not able to resume making payments at the time you are supposed to do so. The best thing you can do is pick up the telephone and call your creditor _before the payment is due_ and explain to them, with complete honestly, calmly and without profanity, what has happened and when you expect you will be able to meet your financial obligation. _Do not_ tell them you will make the payment in a week _unless you are **absolutely sure** you will be able to do so_. Your honesty and good credibility with your creditor are the reasons your creditor is willing to work with

---

[14] _I once saw a poster, stating there were three kinds of people: Those who make things happen; those who watch things happen; and those who wonder what happened. By preparing a financial analysis for your present condition and contacting your creditors promptly, you will be one of the people that "make things happen." It will be good things. Creditors will almost always work with you. People who fail to take these steps will be among those who "watch things happen" or "wonder what happened." People who do not notify their creditors of their financial problems in advance of their becoming behind in payments, or who are not truthful with their creditors, or who fail to respond to creditor's telephone calls and letters, are likely candidates for having their house foreclosed, car repossessed, and face law suits from their creditors._

you. Don't destroy it. If you tell a creditor you will make a payment in two weeks and you make the payment in two weeks, you will look like a hero. If you promise to make a payment in one week but don't do so until the second week, though, you will look like an unreliable, dishonest person to a creditor.

Creditors really do not want to repossess your car, or foreclose on your house, or file a law suit against you. They are not in business to do that. They are in the money business. But if a creditor is not told of your situation in advance, or you break a promise to them, your credibility with them will be damaged. They will feel they are at high risk of your not paying your debt. They will then act to protect their interest.

You will probably experience telephone calls from each creditor every day or two. _Do not avoid their calls._ Talk _with_ them (not at them) – calmly, candidly, without anger, sarcasm or profanity. Tell them the truth. _Do not_ make a promise to make a payment unless you know definitely when you will be able to do so. And keep a written record for each creditor of when you talked with them, with whom you talked, and exactly what was said, especially any promises that were made. Keep these records near the telephone, and review them each day to make sure you make any promised payments on time, make promised telephone calls on time, etc.

All communications with creditors need to be polite, calm, without sarcasm or profanity, and with complete honesty. Yelling profanities at a creditor will accomplish nothing good, and may destroy your credibility and the opportunity to have that creditor work with you. You will find that almost all creditors – including the Internal Revenue Service – will work with you and treat you with respect and consideration if you are honest with them and treat them with respect and consideration.

Once in a while, you will come into contact with a creditor who will be belligerent, or rude, or demand payments you cannot possibly make, or perhaps even use profanities. Keep your cool. Be totally honest. Don't lower yourself to responding with profanities or yelling. And above all, do not make any promises on payment unless you are absolutely sure you can keep the promise. If the creditor continues to be hostile, calmly ask, "May I have your name again please? And may I speak with your supervisor?"

Often, a creditor will then begin to act respectfully and courteously when you have continued to act courteously throughout the conversation. And possibly your conversation is being recorded. He will not want you to talk to his supervisor and have him hear the recorded conversation.

Keep in mind creditors hear all kinds of excuses on why people cannot pay their bills. Many are as phony as a three dollar bill. Creditors are naturally skeptical of reasons for non-payment of bills. You need to establish credibility with your creditors. It begins with your contacting them *before* you are behind in payments. It continues with your communicating with them regularly; always being totally honest with them; always remaining calm and talking with them without profanities; and doing exactly what you promise them you will do, on time.

CHAPTER 9

HEADS I WIN; TAILS YOU LOSE

The business practices of the housing industry could well be titled, "heads I win, tails you lose." Lets look first at a typical sale of a $180,000 house where everything goes well. The house buyer agrees to purchase a house for $180,000, which is the value assigned to it by the appraiser hired by the mortgage company. The buyer pays a 10% down payment ($18,000), and agrees to pay the mortgage company a certain monthly payment, which includes monthly premiums of about $50 for PMI (private mortgage insurance), and accepts a homeowner's warranty required by the mortgage company at closing. At closing, the closing attorney pays the seller $180,000 less the realtor's fee of $10,800 (6% of the sale price) and less any mortgage balance the seller has due on the house; pays $10,800 to the realtor; pays off the seller's mortgage company; pays $4,860 to a mortgage broker for a loan origination fee; $2,592 to the buyer's mortgage company for an administration fee; $300 to an appraiser for his appraisal of the house; $400 to himself as closing attorney; and some $2,632 in other fees to other parties. The new buyer pays $10,784 in closing costs plus the $18,000 down payment, making this total payment at closing $28,784. No serious problems arise with the house. The new owners have steady income, pay their mortgage payments on time, and live in their house for many years. Everyone is happy. The mortgage company says, "I win."

In the second case where a buyer purchases an identical house with identical price, closing expenses, etc., the buyer soon finds his house is a lemon with many serious defects. He tries to get the previous owner (or builder, if it is a new house) to repair the defects – but he refuses. The new owner files a claim with his homeowner's warranty company, but quickly learns they also will do nothing. He then files a law suit against the previous owner (or builder), but his case is thrown out of court because his homeowner's warranty requires binding arbitration (which provided him no help) and forbids a law suit. Then his job requires him to move out of town about two years after his house purchase. He puts his house up for sale. But after being for sale for two years, no one has purchased it, or even made an offer, because of the defects. Quickly, he learns he cannot pay the expenses of living in his new community and continue to pay the mortgage, utilities, insurance, taxes, etc. on his vacant house. He stops making the mortgage payments.

The mortgage company soon forecloses on his house and takes possession, causing him to lose everything he has invested in his house. Eventually, the mortgage company sells his house. Though realtors determined the value of the house was more than $239,000 by their Comparative Market Analysis, the mortgage company found the highest price they could get for the house was $172,000 due to the defects. After paying a realtor $10,320 (6% of the sale price) for their services, the mortgage company realized $161,680 from the sale. With interest and penalties, the former owner owed the mortgage company some $184,000. Hence, the sale of the house brought $22,320 less to the mortgage company than was due them. The mortgage company lost $22,320 on the sale.

Or did they? Remember PMI (private mortgage insurance)? This insurance protects the mortgage company from such losses. PMI will pay the mortgage company for this loss. Who paid the premiums for the PMI insurance? The house owner who just had his house foreclosed. It was a part of his monthly mortgage payments. The mortgage company may well say to the former owner, "heads I win, tails you lose."

If you have already read the Biography in the Appendix, the above may sound familiar. For this is precisely what happened to the author. But the charade does not stop here. In the four years following foreclosure of the author's house, it has been sold *three times.* Assuming it took 180 days for the house to be listed for sale before it was sold each time, that means each of the three newest owners of the house had decided to sell it less than a year after moving in. It smells like the defects of the house were never corrected – only hidden – and each of the new owners became aware of them within a year of living there and decide to move out.

Are people of the housing industry concerned about the author's house being sold over and over? Not a bit. They are probably licking their chops over this "cash cow" that the author's house has become. Assuming an average sale price of $180,000 for each sale of the house, this is approximately what has been paid to the people in the housing industry in the last four years: $32,400 to realtors; $14,580 to mortgage brokers for loan origination fees; $900 to appraisers; $7,776 to mortgage companies for administrative fees (in addition to interest they receive on mortgage payments); and $1,200 to attorneys for closing fees. They are being *rewarded* for churning this house with sale after sale after sale. Heads I win, tails you lose.

Perhaps this is what Mr. Weasel[15] (the attorney for Mr. Herman) meant when he wrote on March 1, 1999 in response to Mr. Herman's previous letter demanding that the judge's summary decision (decision without a trial) for the builder and against Mr. Herman be appealed. Attorney Weasel wrote to Mr. Herman, saying his letter was essentially correct, but not as objective as needed, and he would not appeal the case.

Mr. Herman's objective was simply to obtain justice; to have the builder correct the defects. In 1999, he did not realize his house was going to become a cash cow for certain parties in the housing industry. Shame on Mr. Herman for

---

[15] *Not the true name of this person*

expecting attorney Weasel to vigorously present Herman's case in court and expecting justice. See Biography in the Appendix for more details.

Attorney Weasel never explained how Mr. Herman's factual assessment could have been more objective. One is inclined to wonder if, in reality, attorney Weasel was saying Mr. Herman was not being objective in expecting justice. Consider these facts:

1. Mr. Herman's house was built with many defects. Some of the defects were documented in writing by the builder's suppliers three months before the house was completed. The builder knew, or should have known, of these defects prior to completion of the house.

2. Attorney Weasel was informed that Ms. Donna Jackal[16], mortgage loan officer at Griffin Federal Savings Bank, had required Mr. Herman to purchase a homeowner's warranty, stating that it was required by the Veteran's Administration – when, in fact the Veteran's Administration never required a homeowner's warranty.[17] Attorney Weasel was given the letter sent by the Veterans Administration to Mr. Herman, stating that a homeowner's warranty was not required to obtain a VA Guaranteed Loan. But when attorney Weasel deposed Mr. John Swindler[18] (the builder), and Mr. Swindler stated the Veterans Administration required a homeowner's warranty, attorney Weasel did not challenge him on this or present the letter from the Veteran's Administration. Attorney Weasel also failed to ask builder Swindler if he had paid anyone, or done any favors for mortgage officer Donna Jackal or anyone else at Griffin Federal Savings Bank, to induce her or the bank to require Mr. Herman to purchase a

---

[16] *Not the true name of this person*
[17] *The homeowner's warranty had the effect of protecting builder Swindler from a law suit from Mr. Herman. See Biography in Appendix for details.*
[18] *Not the true name of this person*

homeowner's warranty under false pretenses. Attorney Weasel also failed to ask builder Swindler if he had paid, or done any favors for, anyone on the Fayette County Building Inspection Department to induce them to issue a Certificate of Occupancy for Mr. Herman's house when, in fact, the house did not comply with the HUD or Georgia building codes.

3. Attorney Weasel adamantly refused to depose mortgage officer Donna Jackal, or anyone at Griffin Federal Savings Bank, to: (a) ask why they required Mr. Herman to purchase a homeowner's warranty under the false claim that it was required by the Veteran's Administration; (b) ask if builder Swindler had paid anyone anything, or done any favors for anyone, at Griffin Federal Savings Bank to induce them to require Mr. Herman to purchase a homeowner's warranty under false pretenses.

4. Attorney Weasel was informed there were two Licensed Professional Engineers and many building suppliers prepared to testify on the house defects in Mr. Herman's behalf, as well as the Veteran's Administration. Attorney Weasel conveyed this information to the Superior Court of Fayette County. After presenting all of the evidence, it is believed the jury would have found totally for Mr. Herman and, perhaps, added punitive damages against builder Swindler and Griffin Federal Savings Bank for fraudulent conduct. Also, the Fayette County Building Department may have been asked in court why they issued a Certificate of Occupancy for a house that did not comply with HUD or Georgia building codes, and why had they refused to act on the matter or respond to Mr. Herman when he informed them. The jury might have also assessed some damages against the county for the conduct of the Building Department.

5. Mr. Herman's house was located near Fayetteville, Georgia in Fayette County. Fayetteville is a small city 37 miles southwest of Atlanta. If this case had been allowed to go to trial and the jury decision was in favor of Mr. Herman,

it could have been very costly for builder Swindler and Griffin Federal Savings Bank, and hurt their businesses. It would have also been embarrassing to the Fayette County Building Department, and could have cost the county money if the jury had assessed damages to them.

6. In October of 1998, attorney Weasel had told Mr. Herman there would be a jury trial in March of 1999, and he would notify Mr. Herman of the exact date when the Court informed him. When Mr. Herman had not heard from attorney Weasel by February of 1999, he called attorney Weasel. Only then did attorney Weasel inform him that the Fayette County Superior Court had awarded a summary judgment for builder Swindler and against Mr. Herman *26 days earlier.* Mr. Herman immediately instructed attorney Weasel to appeal the case. On March 1, 1999, attorney Weasel notified Mr. Herman he had decided not to appeal the case. His notification was three days *after* the deadline to appeal. In short, attorney Weasel made sure Mr. Herman could not appeal his case with another attorney.

7. Attorney Weasel's office is in Fayetteville. He depends upon the people and businesses in that small community for his legal practice. If he had successfully presented Mr. Herman's case and prevailed in court, it would have been at the expense of other businesses and prominent people in Fayetteville, possibly to the detriment of his business.

8. The judges in Georgia are elected to office. If Mr. Herman's case were to go to trial and a jury award damages to Mr. Herman (who, by 1999, had moved from his Fayetteville home) at the expense of a local bank, builder, and possibly other Fayetteville parties, this could have hurt his chances for re-election.

Mr. Herman's case of being denied justice by the legal system is not at all unique. In fact, it is frighteningly common.

In 1993, Ms. Cynthia Ramada[19] of the Poconos of Pennsylvania wrote to the Pennsylvania Attorney General about what she felt was a conspiracy between mortgage companies, banks, builders and appraisers in her area creating fictitiously high house appraisals to enable them to get high price mortgages on poorly constructed houses, such as hers, and asked for help. The Attorney General's office responded there was nothing they could do.

By 2001, the number of irate people in her area with the same complaint had grown to more than 600. Now the Attorney General's office was ready to listen. Investigators have found that builders and mortgage companies were offering bribes to appraisers to inflate the appraisals on houses. If the appraisers balked, they were threatened.

A brief surf on the internet showed there are many, many appraisers being arrested and losing their licenses for inflating appraisals in every state. Why were they inflating appraisals? It was due to pressure, intimidation and threats from mortgage companies and builders.

A brief look on the internet shows there are many mortgage companies and banks who have been found to have committed fraud. And in the news on August 10, 2003, the investigation in the Enron Corporation scandal claims the Enron deception of investors and employees was done with the help of some of the largest banks in the world where they made secret side deals with Enron executives, including J.P. Morgan Chase, Citigroup, and Merrill Lynch. These three banks have already contributed more than 300 million dollars to a restitution fund for the wrongdoings of their executives.

Clearly, there are banks, builders and mortgage companies which are not above offering bribes, intimidating people,

---

[19] *Not the true name of this person.*

threatening people, lying or committing fraud if it will produce more profit for them.

Ms. Donna Jackal, mortgage officer of Griffin Federal Savings Bank, called the author one day with no advance notice and told him to go to the closing attorney's office immediately and close on his house loan.[20] He balked, and reminded her that she had not provided closing papers in advance for him to review and had not given advance notice of the closing date, as she had promised. She then threatened to increase his interest rate if he did not sign the closing papers immediately.[21] Clearly, Ms. Jackal was not above lying or threatening a person. And, presumably, she was acting as instructed by her bank. Heads I win, tails you lose.

Thirdly, lets look at another scenario. Suppose a house buyer purchases a house that is appraised at $180,000 by the appraiser hired by the mortgage company. The house buyer agrees to pay $180,000. They move into the house and live there with no problems, paying the monthly mortgage faithfully. After five years, they find it necessary to move. They put their house up for sale. In a new appraisal, it is appraised at $179,000. The owners are shocked that their house has not appreciated in value. The realtor, the mortgage company, and the appraiser all say it is due to the poor economy, other local conditions, etc. The house owners accept this and proceed to sell their house for $179,000. They then think nothing more of this.

Perhaps, in some cases, a poor economy, etc. are the culprits. But in other cases, the initial appraisal may have been the culprit. Suppose the true appraisal value of their house was $150,000 when they bought it, but the appraiser

---

[20] *Griffin Federal Savings Bank no longer exists as a separate bank. It was purchased by Regions Bank*

[21] *See Biography in the Appendix for details.*

tacked on another $30,000 due to pressure from the mortgage company and/or seller.

The house buyers never knew this – and will never learn this. The mortgage company, consequently, was able to sell a mortgage for $30,000 more than if the house had been honestly appraised, earning them more interest. For example, from Table 3, their monthly mortgage payments with a 7% thirty year mortgage of $150,000 would have been $1,000. With a $180,000 mortgage at the same interest rate, their monthly mortgage payments would have been $1,200. If the house owners had fully paid the mortgage over thirty years, the mortgage company would have collected $72,000 more than if the house had been honestly appraised! Heads I win, tails you lose.

One may be inclined to ask why Congress is doing nothing to stop this crime. It appears there are two reasons. First, Congress may not be aware of this. Very few of the people scammed become aware of their being scammed. So there are probably very few complaints being sent to Congressmen. Perhaps this book should be sent to each of the 535 members of Congress so they will become informed. No, make that 534. There's no sense in sending a book to Congressman Zell Miller from Georgia. Mr. Miller was informed of the housing fraud experienced by the author in Georgia while Mr. Miller was governor of that state. His office responded, saying the information the author had submitted appears to show that a possible violation of the law(s) administered by this office has occurred. However, they refused to investigate this matter or take any action.

The second key reason is believed to be pressure from the banking and mortgage company lobbies. Indeed, Congress is currently considering changing the bankruptcy laws so that a person filing for bankruptcy _cannot have credit card debts forgiven!_ Heads I win, tails you lose.

141

The purpose of this chapter is to make the reader fully aware of what is happening in the housing industry. There is only one party vitally interested in your welfare. That is you. It is extremely important for a house buyer to form their own team of experts to guide them through the building and purchasing of a house. Your team will know who the honest people are, and who to avoid. They will recognize scams, unreasonable prices, and unfair business practices. They will level the playing field to enable you to obtain a quality house at a fair price.

CHAPTER 10

SUMMARY

The purchase of a house is the most expensive investment ever made by most people. It is also the most complex. This combination has attracted a number of dishonest people who have devised numerous schemes to scam house buyers. To avoid being scammed, a buyer would need to be an expert in real estate, appraising, law, building codes, house construction and inspection, and in finance, as well as an excellent negotiator. Since none of us possess all these skills, and since the average person purchases only two or three houses in their lifetime and cannot devote their life to becoming an expert in all of these fields, one needs to assemble a team, each of whom is an expert in one of these fields. It has been shown that failure to form a team for the building and purchase of a house by a well-educated engineer and businessman resulted in his being fleeced – and that this is happening to thousands of other house buyers each day.

The reader is shown, while in the privacy of their home, how to analyze if investing in a house is appropriate for them, and if so, what price house is appropriate for their financial position.

The reader is presented plans on how to form a team to purchase or build a house, and how to accomplish their goals and avoid the costly traps and scams.

Certain features of a house profoundly affect the cost of house ownership and the comfort, safety and security of owners, but often receive little or no consideration. They have been presented here for the reader's consideration.

In spite of the best planning and preparation, a financial crisis can – and does – strike house owners each day. The reader is shown how this can happen, and how to navigate through these troubled waters.

By following the plans set forth in this book, the reader will be able to purchase the house that he/she desires with the best opportunity of avoiding a financial crisis and their home becoming a dream home.

APPENDIX

BIOGRAPHY

Charles A. Herman, author of this book, holds a Bachelor of Science in Mechanical Engineering degree plus one year of graduate work. He also has a Master of Science in Business Administration degree, specializing in finance. He was a Licensed Professional Engineer for thirty-three years until his recent retirement. He was also Chief Engineer of three companies and President/CEO of three companies. In these capacities, he has written many technical articles and presented numerous seminars. He has also been awarded one patent, and received awards for many other inventions.

During his career, his peers appointed him to several unique positions (for example, one of three engineers appointed to the Advanced Concepts Group by Navistar Truck Engineering Center where design, development and testing of products for vehicles ten years in the future were conducted; one of three engineers appointed by the Ambulance Manufacturing Division of the National Truck Equipment Association to work with Ford Motor Company on fuel system problems on Ford vehicles used for Ambulances; and appointed Chairman of the Technical Committee for six years by the Ambulance Manufacturers' Division with the responsibility of writing national performance specifications for ambulances). The reasons they cited for these appointments were his skills in mechanical engineering, electrical engineering, and the ability and tenacity to carry projects through to successful conclusions.

During his career, he has purchased six houses, and managed apartments for four years. In 1994, he and his wife decided to build their "dream house" (Figure 12) in the country seven miles from Fayetteville, Georgia. It was a 2,800 square foot, two story, four bedroom brick house located on a 4.7 acre heavily wooded lot, which included flowering dogwood trees and a natural stream. It was to be their home for the rest of their lives.

Though Mr. Herman had an excellent education and many years of business and engineering experience, he made many mistakes in purchasing and having his house built. He placed way too much trust in the people responsible for building and financing his house. *He did not adequately investigate the general contractor or the house documents, and did not retain a personal attorney, architect or house inspector prior to building the house.* This cost him dearly. His errors are shown in underlined italics.

Figure 12

The general contractor selected was Mr. John Swindler[22], a house contractor in Fayetteville, Georgia. A check with the Better Business Bureau and the state of Georgia showed there were no complaints against him. He provided references of people he had built houses for previously. In meetings with

---

[22] *Not the true name of this person.*

them and looking over their houses, the author found the people were satisfied with Mr. Swindler's work, had no complaints about their houses, and he observed no problems. *The word of Mr. Swindler's references were accepted without asking the references for other references. Naturally, Mr. Swindler used references he knew would speak favorably of him and probably omitted anyone who had problems with their house. If the author had asked Mr. Swindler's references for the names of other people for whom Mr. Swindler had built houses, he may have found houses poorly built by Mr. Swindler.*

The mortgage company chosen was Griffin Federal Savings Bank[23] of Griffin, Georgia, where the author had his checking and savings accounts. The loan officer was Ms. Donna Jackal,[24] whose office was located in Fayetteville.

Mr. Swindler was given a floorplan drawing for the house created by Mr. Herman. Mr. Swindler, in turn, had his architect make the detailed floorplan, structural, electrical, and plumbing drawings for the house. *Though the author checked the architect's floorplan drawing to assure the rooms were laid out as desired, he did not check the other drawings for electrical service, plumbing, etc. He trusted Mr. Swindler and his architect to do what was right, use good building practices, and to comply with local, state and federal HUD building codes.*

Ms. Donna Jackal, the loan officer, established a construction loan which would allow Mr. Swindler to receive "draw" payments as certain milestones were reached in the construction of the house. *She asked the author if he would let Mr. Swindler work directly with the bank and the bank's house inspector to receive the draw payments (partial payment for the construction of the house as Mr. Swindler completed the*

---

[23] *Griffin Federal Savings Bank no longer exists as a separate bank. It was sold to Regions Bank.*
[24] *Not the true name of this person.*

house to certain milestones) without Mr. Herman personally inspecting the house. She assured Mr. Herman that the bank's house inspector would inspect the house to assure work had been completed to each construction milestone and that all work would be in compliance with all building codes and good workmanship standards before the bank would release a draw to Mr. Swindler (the author had not hired his own house inspector). The author agreed to this.

As the house was being constructed, the author noticed that 14 gage wiring was being used for most of the house. Normally, the heavier 12 gage wiring is used – but of course, the lighter 14 gage wire chosen by the builder was less costly and easier to install. The National Electrical Code required that 14 gage wiring be protected by a 15 amp circuit breaker while 12 gage wiring could be protected with a 20 amp circuit breaker. Hence, by using 14 gage wiring and 15 amp circuit breakers, it would not be possible to plug in a crock pot, coffee pot and food warmers into one circuit – it would overload the circuit and trip the circuit breaker. Or plugging in an electric frying pan and almost any other appliance would cause a circuit breaker to trip. Using 12 gage wiring with 20 amp circuit breakers would have prevented this problem. The author asked Mr. Swindler about this. Mr. Swindler claimed the wiring met the standards of Fayette County – but when pressed further, he admitted the wiring did not comply with the building codes of neighboring counties. *The author asked Mr. Swindler to change the wiring from 14 gage to 12 gage. Mr. Swindler said he would do so, but it would cost an additional $900. But the author did not have an additional $900. Hence, the house was built largely with 14 gage wire and 15 amp circuit breakers. If the author had carefully checked the electrical drawings for the house (or had hired an architect or house inspector to examine the drawings), this problem would not have occurred.*

As construction of the house neared completion in November of 1994, the author asked Ms. Jackal about the closing papers and the closing date. She replied the papers would be sent to him, and she would call and provide the closing date in advance of the closing date. *In the meantime, she said the author should go ahead and move into the house upon its completion, which would be prior to the closing.*

Around December 1, 1994, Ms. Jackal called and asked the author to come into her office for a meeting. Upon arriving, he found Mr. Swindler was also there. Ms. Jackal said that the author would need to purchase a home owner's warranty, stating it was required by the Veteran's Administration (the author had a Veterans Administration guaranteed loan). When he explained that he did not know what a home owner's warranty was or where to obtain one, Mr. Swindler said he knew how to obtain it. *The author accepted Ms. Jackal's statement as a fact that the warranty was required by the Veteran's Administration without checking with the Veterans Administration, and allowed Mr. Swindler to obtain the warranty.*

When the house was completed on December 10, 1994, the author and his wife moved in.

At 4:00 P.M. on Thursday, December 29, 1994, Ms. Jackal called, saying that the author must be in the offices of McNally, Fox & Cameron (the closing attorneys) within one hour and close the loan with the bank. The author objected, stating that the closing papers had not been provided in advance for his review, as she had promised; no copy of the warranty had been provided; no advance notice of the closing time was provided, as she had promised; and that he had other commitments at that time. She responded that he needed to be in the attorney's office within one hour and close on the loan or the interest rate would be increased! *With reluctance, he went to the attorney's office and closed the loan. Neither Ms. Jackal or Mr. Swindler, or any other representative of the builder or bank, was present. The only person present was the closing attorney, who Mr. Herman thought was representing him since he was paying the closing attorney.*

Within six weeks after closing, major defects began to appear in the house, including a leaking roof; cracking walls; bricks coming off the front of the house; a well that would run out of water; and well pump controls that burned up frequently. It was subsequently discovered the well and the pump system did not comply with Georgia building codes or the codes required by the Department of Housing and Urban Development – and documentation showed the general contractor knew this or should have known this three months prior to completion of the house. It was also later discovered the driveway was incorrectly located such that a portion of it was located on the neighbor's property.

For more than a year, the author repeatedly requested Mr. Swindler to repair the defects – but he refused. The author filed a warranty claim – but the warranty provided for the builder to be the warrantor for the first two years. This was appealed to binding arbitration (as required by the warranty). On September 26, 1996, Mr. William Pander[25] appeared at the author's house claiming to be the independent arbitrator appointed by the warranty company. He observed the cracked walls, damage from roof leaks, loose bricks, a well that ran out of water, etc. Later, Mr. Pander ruled that the builder was not responsible for repairing any of the defects! It turns out Mr. Pander was also a general contractor who built houses!

When later discussed with a veteran Fayetteville realtor, he said it was common operating procedure for home warranty companies to hire house contractors to act as "independent arbitrators", and had seen only one homeowner who had been awarded anything by a warranty company in eleven years.

---

[25] *Not the true name of this person.*

The author contacted the Veteran's Administration and asked for assistance in enforcing the warranty that they had required him to purchase, according to Ms. Jackal, mortgage officer at Griffin Federal Savings Bank. <u>The Veteran's Administration responded that they did not require the purchase of the homeowner's warranty! Hence, Ms. Jackal had deliberately misrepresented to the author that the Veteran's Administration required a homeowner's warranty in order to obtain a V.A. guaranteed loan.</u>

In looking back, it is apparent that Mr. Swindler, the general contractor, knowingly and deliberately built the house substandard and in violation of state and federal building codes to cut his expenses and increase his profit. It is believed he and Ms. Jackal, the loan officer at Griffin Federal Savings Bank, conspired to require the author to purchase a homeowner's warranty, stating falsely that the Veteran's Administration required it. The homeowner's warranty had the effect of protecting Mr. Swindler from having to repair defects since (1) the warranty stated the builder was the warrantor for the first two years, (2) if there was a disagreement between the homeowner and the builder, it had to be settled by an "independent" arbitrator (who turned out to be another general contractor – typical, according to a veteran realtor in Fayetteville), and (3) the warranty required binding arbitration, preventing the homeowner from seeking justice in the court.

The author contacted Mr. James S. Cameron, the attorney at McNally, Fox & Cameron, where the closing of the house loan had been conducted, and requested Mr. Cameron to represent him in legal action against Mr. Swindler to enforce correction of the builder's defects in the author's new house. But Mr. Cameron declined, stating it would be a "conflict of interest." *<u>In other words, the attorney the author thought was **his** closing attorney was not **his** attorney at all. He was an attorney for the bank and, possibly, Mr. Swindler, and was</u>*

*looking out for **their** interests at loan closing– not those of the author.*

Subsequently, the author retained Mr. Weasel, an attorney in Fayetteville, and filed suit against Mr. Swindler.

Naturally, attorney Weasel was supplied with all documentation and was informed of everything. In particular, attorney Weasel was informed by the author that he believed Ms. Jackal and Mr. Swindler had committed fraud and conspired to commit fraud by stating the Veterans Administration required the author to purchase a homeowner's warranty, when in fact the Veterans Administration did not require a warranty, and sent a letter stating this.

Attorney Weasel's letter of October 13, 1998 indicated there would be a jury trial in March of 1999. In a telephone conversation with attorney Weasel in January of 1999, he confirmed again to the author that there would be a jury trial in March, and would call the author when he learned the date.

When the author had not heard from attorney Weasel by February 22, 1999, he called him. Only then did attorney Weasel inform the author that, on January 27, 1999 (26 days earlier), the Fayette County Superior Court Judge had ruled for summary judgment in favor of Mr. Swindler because there was a homeowner's warranty. The judge had ignored the fact that the author had been fraudulently induced to purchase the warranty and that by law, the author had the right to revoke the warranty.

The author immediately instructed attorney Weasel verbally to appeal the decision. He then sent a letter to attorney Weasel, again instructing him to appeal the decision to the Appellate Court. The author cited numerous court cases where a party had been fraudulently induced into a contract and the courts consistently ruled the fraudulently induced party had the right to void the contract. Complete information was provided on these cases so attorney Weasel could easily look them up and use them as references in his appeal.

On March 1, 1999, attorney Weasel wrote to the author, stating the author was correct for the most part but his factual assessment was less objective than it needed to be. He then ended his letter by saying he was refusing to appeal the case. Attorney Weasel's letter was written three days after the deadline for Mr. Herman to appeal his case, making it impossible to hire another attorney and appeal.

Consequently, the author was stuck with a new house with many serious defects; a builder who would not correct the defects; a legal system which would not bring about justice; and inadequate money to make the needed repairs, estimated at approximately $20,000. To further complicate matters, the author's company went out of business. When he was unable to find work within commuting distance of his home, he was forced to accept a position 285 miles away in Huntsville, Alabama.

The Fayetteville, Georgia house was placed for sale, and remained for sale for almost two years. But there were no offers due to the obvious defects. For twenty months, the author was living and working in Huntsville, Alabama while owning a house in Fayetteville, Georgia, trying to maintain it, and paying mortgage payments, utilities, insurance, etc. The expenses far exceeded the author's income. Clearly, he was well on the way to bankruptcy. Upon the advice of attorney Weasel, the author ceased making mortgage payments on the Fayetteville house. In time, the mortgage company foreclosed on the house, causing the author to lose everything he had invested in the house and damaging his credit. Eventually, the mortgage company sold the house for $172,000 – way below the mortgage amount and the $239,900 the house was valued at by realtors.

During the more than three years the author was trying to enforce repair of builder's defects on his house, he was also in contact with other parties, including Mr. Zell Miller, then Governor of Georgia.[26] Upon reviewing the documents the author presented, the Governor's office responded by letter on August 15, 1996, stating the information the author had submitted appeared to show that a possible violation of the law(s) has occurred. However, they refused to take any action. The Fayetteville Building Inspection Department refused to explain how a house clearly in violation of building codes was approved by their department – and needless to say, took no action to bring about correction of the defects. The Veteran's Administration also provided no assistance. The documentation was also presented to *The Wall Street Journal* and *The Atlanta Journal Constitution* newspapers and "The I Team", an investigative news team on television channel 5 in Atlanta, Georgia. The newspapers did not respond. "The I Team" did respond, stating they had previously presented an expose' on housing fraud, and found fraud so widespread and commonplace that it was not newsworthy.

Upon reflecting on this, and the fact that he had more than eight years of college education and thirty-two years of professional experience in industry and was defrauded and denied legal recourse, in spite of more than three years of dogged persistence, the author felt there may well be many more people in "the same boat." He learned that 1 ½% to 2% of house mortgages each year end up in foreclosure. Since there were 6,213,000 mortgages written for houses nationally in 2000, it follows that 93,000 to more than 124,000 families lost their houses to foreclosure in that one year. Without question, many hundreds of thousands of other families were threatened with foreclosure. And probably many more hundreds of thousands of other families were stuck with poorly or fraudulently constructed houses with defects and no legal recourse, and predatory mortgages, but were able to pay

---

[26] *Mr. Zell Miller no longer is Governor of Georgia. He is now a Congressman representing Georgia.*

their mortgages. Though it was not possible to determine how many people lost their houses or suffered grief due to poorly or fraudulently constructed houses or predatory mortgages, it is believed hundreds of thousands of people are victims of these practices each year.

A wise businessman once said, "When life deals you a lemon, make lemonade!" This book is the author's "lemonade." It is dedicated to helping people avoid the nightmare of purchasing a fraudulently or poorly constructed house; having fraudulent or unjust business practices thrust upon them by realtors, appraisers, house builders or mortgage companies; and showing how to purchase a house safely and wisely.

INDEX

A

Air Quality Control 79
Appreciation Of Real Estate 18
Associations And Covenants 95

B

Basement
    Flooded 5
    House 82
Bathroom Design 80, 84, 90, 99, 105, 109
Budget 33, 43, 161

C

Carbon Monoxide Detectors 109, 110
Ceiling Fans 85
Closets 86
Closing 3, 59, 161, 162
Crawl Space 82, 118, 163

E

Electrical Generator 86

F

Financial Preparation 55
Fire Extinguishers 110
Fireplace 88

G

Garage
    Construction 65
    Safety 89, 111
    Security 111

H

Handicap Provisions 90
Heating And Air Conditioning 83, 91
Homeowner Associations And Covenants 95
Homeowner's Warranty 73, 162, 164
House Appraiser 57, 161
House Inspector 3, 56, 69, 164

Housing Fraud In The Poconos 58, 139

K

Keyless Entry 115
Kitchen Design 96

L

Lighting 99
Lightning Protection 115

M

Mortgage Pre-Approval 56, 71
Mortgage Pre-Qualification 55, 71

N

Negotiating Price And Closing Costs 6

P

Paint 99
Pool And Jacuzzi
    Construction 100
    Safety 122
Private Mortgage Insurance 19, 20, 25, 101, 165

R

Radon Gas 118
Realtor
    Buyer's 54, 63, 161
    Seller's 4, 54, 165
Roof Design 101

S

Security Lights 119
Security System 119
Shape Of Your House 102
Slab House 82, 165
Surge Suppression 120
    See Lightning Protection 115

T

Table 1
   Typical Expenses Incurred In Purchasing An Existing $180,000 House With A 10% Down Payment 3
Table 2
   How To Determine The Maximum Monthly Mortgage Payment Allowed By A Mortgage Company 9
Table 3
   Thirty Year Mortgage For A Given Monthly Payment And Interest Rate 12
Table 4
   Typical Expenses Incurred In Selling A House Purchased For $180,000 Two Years Earlier 18
Table 5
   Total Cost To Purchase A $180,000 House And Own It For Two Years 19
Table 6
   Total Future Financial Analysis 29
Table 7
   Current Financial Budget 37
Table 8
   Monthly Budget Expense Form 44
Table 9
   Monthly Budget Expense Form - July 45
Table 10
   Monthly Budget Expense Form - August 47
Table 11
   Monthly Budget Expense Form - August 48
Table 12
   Monthly Budget Expense Form - September 50
Table 13
   Savings For Anticipated Future Expenses 51
Telephone Junction Box 122
Thermostat 93
   Automatic 94

V

Veterans Administration Guaranteed Loans 103, 136, 149

W

Warranty Bond 166
    See House Warranty 164
Water Heater 82, 85, 104
Water Pipe Insulation 105
Windows 105, 123

Y

Yard Watering Systems 107

GLOSSARY

Appraiser: One who is licensed by a city or state as being trained and qualified to place an estimated value on a house.

Architect: A professional licensed to design buildings and houses and to oversee their construction.

Budget: A financial plan showing what the projected incomes and expenses will be over a period of time.

Buyer's Realtor: A licensed realtor hired by a house buyer to assist in the purchase of a house.

Central Sprinkler System: A lawn watering system wherein sprinkler heads are permanently installed in the lawn slightly lower than the surface of the grass and connected to underground pipes, enabling uniform lawn watering without the use of hoses and sprinklers.

Certificate of Occupancy: A document written by a city or county which certifies that: (1) a permit has been issued for the construction of a house at a particular location; (2) the house has been constructed in accordance with the plans and specifications submitted to the city or county; (3) the house complies with all the building laws and zoning ordinances; (4) and that the house is approved for use.

Closing: The concluding action in the purchase of a house. A meeting, typically with the seller, buyer, seller's realtor, buyer's realtor and attorney, and closing attorney wherein appropriate documents are signed, transferring ownership of a house from the seller to the buyer, with the buyer paying any required down payment and closing costs, and agreeing to pay a mortgage company a certain monthly payment for the house. The seller receives payment for the house at this meeting.

Closing Attorney: An attorney who chairs the closing on a house. This attorney makes sure all required documents are present, correct, and properly signed, dated and notarized; that each party that is to receive a payment (e.g., the seller) is properly paid; and that any payments due from the buyer are received.

Closing Costs: The costs incurred at closing. Typically, they include the appraiser's fee, loan origination fee to a broker, administrative fee to a mortgage company, interest on mortgage from date of closing to date of first mortgage payment, closing fee for the title company, title insurance, recording fee, closing attorney fee, down payment, and possibly other miscellaneous charges. Costs may also include fees for your buyer's realtor, your personal attorney, and your house inspector, or these parties may bill you separately. See Table 1 on page 3.

Comparative Market Analysis: Often abbreviated "CMA". A comparison of a specific house to other similar houses in the same area that have recently been sold, with the intent to determine the fair market value of the specific house. It is presumed the fair market value of a specific house will be the same as the selling price of similar houses sold in the area, with adjustments made for variations between the specific house and the houses sold. Appraisers and real estate agents typically perform comparative market analyses for house buyers and sellers.

Consequential Damage: Damage that occurs as a consequence of some action. For example, a house with a roof leak may incur water damage on inside walls and carpets. The damage to the inside walls and carpets would be consequential damage. Often, consequential damage is not covered in a homeowner's warranty.

Construction Loan: A temporary loan from a mortgage company in which the mortgage company pays a builder certain amounts of money during the construction of a house. Upon completion of the house, the construction loan is often rolled into the mortgage loan.

Covenant: Contract. An agreement in writing.

Crawl Space House: A house which has a space between its ground floor and the ground. Typically, this space is about three feet high. A house which has a perimeter foundation, but no basement or concrete inside the perimeter foundation.

Creditor: One who loans money. One to whom money is due.

Credit Report: A written report from a credit bureau which contains a record of all credit transactions for a person or company, showing all on-time payments, late payments, and non-payments of obligations.

General Contractor: Person or company who has been assigned and accepted overall responsibility for the construction of a house.

Geothermal Heat Pump: A heat pump which has a heat exchanger buried deep underground to collect heat from the ground and pump it into a house. It utilizes only electricity. It is an extremely clean and economical method of heating a house, but also very expensive to install.

Heat Pump: A house heating system which literally pumps heat into the house from the air outside a house. It is a very clean and efficient means of heating a house when the outside air temperature is about 35 degrees F or warmer. At lower temperatures, the outside air does not have sufficient heat to heat the house, thereby requiring an auxiliary heater in the heat pump to turn on (the auxiliary heater may be electric or gas). The efficiency decreases as the temperature decreases below about 35 degrees F and the auxiliary heater is required to produce more and more heat. The heat pump utilizes only electricity (except the auxiliary heater, which may be electric or gas).

House Inspector: One who is licensed by a city or state as being experienced, qualified and trustworthy of inspecting a house for defects and writing an accurate report.

House Warranty: A warranty which, in theory, is supposed to protect a house buyer from defects in a newly constructed house. In reality, it is often worded in a manner which protects the builder from being held responsible for defects and poor workmanship, and prohibits a home owner from seeking justice in court.

Mortgage: Document by which the ownership of a house is conditionally transferred to a creditor (e.g., a mortgage company, seller, builder) as security until the mortgage is fully paid by the buyer. Upon full payment of the mortgage, ownership of the house is transferred to the buyer.

Mortgage Broker: An agent who bargains or carries on negotiations with mortgage companies in an effort to find the most favorable mortgage for a buyer.

Pre – Approval: A <u>letter of commitment</u> from a mortgage company to a house buyer, stating that they <u>will approve a mortgage</u> for a specified dollar amount and interest rate for a certain period of time. It is obtained by applying for a mortgage, and the mortgage company undertaking a <u>rigorous</u> evaluation of the application, the applicant's credit history, job history, income tax returns, etc. It is a very rigorous procedure.

Pre – Qualification: A letter or statement from a mortgage company to a house buyer, stating they <u>may</u> be able to provide a mortgage for a specified dollar amount and interest rate for a specified period of time <u>based upon the information provided</u>

to them by the buyer. It is a very casual process, and does not provide a mortgage commitment to the buyer. Its value is in obtaining interest rates from mortgage companies and making comparisons.

Private Mortgage Insurance: Insurance which protects a mortgage company from loss in case of non-payment of a mortgage by a house buyer. Typically, mortgage companies require a house buyer to have private mortgage insurance until the buyer has paid at least 20% of the purchase price. Often abbreviated "PMI".

Property Tax: A tax placed upon real estate by city, county and state governments.

Seller's Realtor: A realtor who works for a house owner by presenting his/her house for sale to potential buyers. The seller's realtor is normally paid a percentage of the sale price by the seller.

Slab House: A house which is built on a continuous slab of concrete under the ground floor with no basement. Typically, the first floor tile and carpeting are applied directly on top of the concrete slab.

Subcontractor: One who contracts with the general contractor to render some performance for which the general contractor is responsible for performing. For example, the general contractor would be responsible for wiring a house he has contracted to build. But the general contractor may not have people with the skills needed to wire the house. Consequently, the general contractor would contract with a subcontractor to do the wiring. The general contractor remains responsible for proper performance of the work of any subcontractor he may hire.

Surveyor: A professional person who is licensed by a state to determine the boundaries of property as well as its elevation.

Title Company: A company that writes titles to real estate; also, performs a title search to insure house and land are clear and free of liens, judgments and mortgages, and that the seller has a right to sell the house.

Title Insurance: Insurance which protects a house buyer in the event a lien, judgment or mortgage exists on a house or land when the title search showed there was no lien, judgment or mortgage on the house or land.

Topography: The surface configuration of land (e.g., hilly, flat, rocky).

Warranty Bond: A written promise under seal from a bonding company which states they will pay legitimate warranty claims up to a specified dollar amount and for a specified period of time in the event the builder of a new house fails or refuses to correct defects reported within a specified period of time. A warranty bond is usually paid for by the builder.